# DAYUMA:
## LIFE UNDER
## WAORANI
## SPEARS

*A Tragedy that Shocked the World.*
*A Vision that Refused to Die.*

# ETHEL EMILY WALLIS

**PUBLISHING**
*A MINISTRY OF YOUTH WITH A MISSION*
P.O. Box 55787, Seattle, WA 98155

YWAM Publishing is the publishing ministry of Youth With A Mission. Youth With A Mission (YWAM) is an international missionary organization of Christians from many denominations dedicated to presenting Jesus Christ to this generation. To this end, YWAM has focused its efforts in three main areas: 1) Training and equipping believers for their part in fulfilling the Great Commission (Matthew 28:19). 2) Personal evangelism. 3) Mercy ministry (medical and relief work).

For a free catalog of books and materials write or call:

YWAM Publishing

P.O. Box 55787, Seattle, WA 98155

(206)771-1153 or (800) 922-2143

e-mail address: 75701.2772 @ compuserve.com

**Dayuma: Life Under Waorani Spears**

Copyright © 1996 **Wycliffe Bible Translators**

Published by YWAM Publishing
P.O. Box 55787, Seattle, WA 98155, USA

Unless otherwise noted, Scripture quotations in this book are taken from the King James Version of the Bible.

Verses marked NIV are taken from the Holy Bible, New Internation Version®, Copyright© 1973, 1978, 1984 by the International Bible Society. Used by permission of Zondervan Publishing House. The "NIV" and "New International Version" trademarks are registered in the United States Patent and Trademark Office by International Bible Society.

ISBN 0-927545-91-8

**Printed in the United States of America.**

# Preface

*Dayuma* by Ethel Emily Wallis describes vividly the years Dayuma tried to forget—days of running and hiding from her people and fearing for her life. It presents a penetrating view of the Waorani people who were feared by outsiders. She shares the difficulties and successes Rachel Saint and Catherine Peeke experienced as they prayed for the opportunity to live and work with the Waorani in order to translate the Scriptures into their language. It is a testimony to the power of prayer and perseverance.

The author added an update of events for this edition. Trying to condense nearly 40 years into a few brief pages presented significant challenges. She sifted through boxes of photographs and files and worked closely with Marj (Saint) Van Der Puy, Mary Sargent, and Steve Saint. I'm grateful to Ethel for setting aside other responsibilities and taking on this assignment wholeheartedly—just as she did in 1959 when she went to the edge of the Waorani jungle to work with Dayuma and Rachel on this book.

The Waorani New Testament, completed in 1992, is a capstone in their history. The Waorani people still face significant challenges in their lives and culture. Many have come to Christ, and they still need our prayers. This story of transformation is being repeated around the world as more and more people receive, read, and understand the gospel in their heart languages. But the work of Bible translation is still far from done. The immediate focus: 1000 languages representing millions of people who do not have God's Word.

I am convinced that Bible translation is the last frontier in missions and the foundation for effective evangelism and church growth. The tragic story of the five young men killed in the

Ecuadorian jungle 40 years ago inspired hundreds of people to proclaim the gospel around the world. We hope and pray that God will use their story and this powerful book again to motivate a new generation to serve the Bible-less peoples of the world.

Hyatt Moore, Director
Wycliffe Bible Translators, USA
May 1996

# Foreword

When Harper and Row first published the hardback edition of *The Dayuma Story* in 1960, it sold over 60,000 copies. Republished in 1971 as a Spire softback, this compelling story was brought to another generation of readers. Now titled *Dayuma*, the book is being rereleased alongside the stage production of the same name. This new, updated version also marks the fortieth anniversary of one of the most enduring stories in modern mission history.

I vividly remember hearing as a young boy the report that five young men had been speared to death by Waorani Indians, known then to the outside world as "Aucas." The story struck a resonating chord in me and, along with others across the world, I prayed that somehow God would provide a way to reach this seemingly "unreachable" people.

God answered those prayers in the form of a young Indian girl. Dayuma became the bridge to her hostile and reclusive people. From the tragic death of five young American missionaries on a small, sandy beach in the Ecuadorian jungle sprang a stunning story of courage, hope, and forgiveness.

Twenty-five years after the killings, my wife and I were invited by Rachel Saint to meet Dayuma. Landing in a muddy jungle clearing that served as a landing strip, we were greeted by the Waorani. Dayuma led us to her open-framed thatched hut. Its sole contents were a hammock, a blowgun, and a jungle radio, together with her two special pets: a parrot and a monkey. We were led through the steamy jungle to the Curaray River and poled downriver to "Palm Beach" in a dugout canoe. Standing with some of the "killers" beside the common grave of the missionaries they had slain, I had the deep conviction that God had not finished with this story yet.

Within a year of that visit to Ecuador, Dayuma and Rachel stayed in our home. They had come to see the Canadian premiere of the stage production *Dayuma*. How would a Waorani Indian woman who had lived her life in the jungle respond to a theatrical experience that portrayed her people, and in which she was the central character?

When the privately arranged preview was over, Dayuma wanted to talk to the cast. As Rachel interpreted, Dayuma related that seeing the reenactment of her life story had challenged her to hurry back to her people so that she could take the Bible, which she called "God's Carving," to the downriver tribes who had not yet heard.

In recent months, Dayuma sent a challenging and timely message from her home in the Ecuadorian rain forest. She said, "There are people in other lands who have not heard yet. Are you going to tell them? You ought to go tell them. Do you understand?" This aging woman of courage calls us to follow her example, to take "God's Carving" to our own "tribe" and then "downriver" to those who have never heard.

I would like to express special thanks and appreciation to Ethel Emily Wallis, for her willingness to update the original manuscript; to Marj Van Der Puy, widow of Nate Saint, for her friendship and unflagging support; for Rachel Saint, now buried with the people she loved and so faithfully served.

Colin Harbinson
Originator and artistic director of the
stage production *Dayuma*
May 1996

## Note to the Reader

Dayuma's people have always called themselves *Waorani* (wah RAH nee), meaning "we the people." Until 1958, this people group living in the Ecuadorian jungle was known to the outside world as *Aucas*, "savages who speared."

In *Dayuma: Life under Waorani Spears*, the glossary, and the prologue written in 1960 by Ethel Emily Wallis, the term *Auca* was retained due to the historic nature of the material.

In 1992 the publication of the New Testament in the Waorani language marked a watershed moment in the history of this people. It was the message of this Book that had rendered obsolete the name *Auca*.

For help in understanding the habitat and unfamiliar names within the tribe, please refer to the glossary and name list found on the final pages of this book.

# Prologue

As I flew in a tiny plane over the Auca forest of terror, deep in eastern Ecuador, to meet Dayuma and Rachel Saint, the reality of a fantastic—but not fictitious—story came alive to me for the first time. Down there, somewhere in that dark greenness stretching endlessly under the tiny plane, Moipa had driven his spears into Tyaento. Tyaento's young daughter Dayuma then fled for her life to the outside, to a jungle hacienda. Eight years later a missionary-linguist found her there carrying heavy loads of bananas from sunrise to sunset, and an incredible story began. I wanted to check the facts before committing them to print.

It was almost dark that September evening when the jungle-hopping plane touched down on the grassy strip chopped out of virgin forest. I was welcomed not only by my good friends Dayuma and Rachel, but also by Dayuma's relative Kimo and his pretty wife, Dawa, Aucas who only a few days before had arrived at the Limoncocha Base of the Wycliffe Bible Translators on their first adventure away from their forest home. Kimo—the muscular young Indian who had participated in the spear-killing of Rachel's brother Nate and four fellow missionaries almost four years earlier! At that moment I felt that I had been dropped into the thick of a thrilling drama.

For more than a month, Rachel and I questioned Kimo and Dawa for confirmation of Dayuma's story. My inability to speak the Auca language was fully compensated for by Rachel's fluency, with satisfying results. Two earlier months in Quito I had devoted all my waking hours to ferreting out the story from documents made available to me: heaps of Rachel's personal letters, reports, and voluminous amounts of Auca text recorded by her since 1955 when she began the study of Dayuma's mother tongue. But I had many queries that were resolved during those unforgettable weeks in the jungle with the Aucas.

Rachel had been asked by Harper & Brothers in 1958 to write this story. But then came an unprecedented invitation to her and Elisabeth Elliot to live in the Aucas' midst—an irresistible opportunity. Living under extremely primitive conditions, with primary concentration on Auca language study, was not an ideal book-writing situation. In July 1959, at the request of Wycliffe director Cameron Townsend, I went to Ecuador to lend Rachel a hand in the project. Although I was reluctant to leave my own work with the Mezquital Otomi Indians of Mexico, I was nevertheless glad to share an assignment with Rachel and thus enable her to continue her work with the Auca tribe in less time out than writing a book involves.

For valuable assistance I am indebted to other Wycliffe colleagues, particularly Catherine Peeke and Nadine Kernodle. Catherine, who speaks Dayuma's second language, Quichua, double-checked crucial points of the story. She also undertook research on the flora and fauna of the Ecuadorian jungle pertinent to the narrative. Her aid on the Glossary is appreciated. Nadine's willing help in the typing of the taped transcriptions for the background material, as well as her careful typing of the manuscript itself, lightened the writing load considerably.

Other Wycliffe members who gave invaluable help were Kenneth Kensinger, Dorothy Jackson, and Katherine Viogtlander.

Dr. Ward Goodenough of the University of Pennsylvania graciously gave valuable suggestions for the preparation of the genealogical materials.

I am also indebted to Eleanor Jordan of Harper & Brothers, and Cornell Capa of Magnum Photos for their valuable and timely help.

And Dayuma herself cooperated unstintingly in the telling of her story, although the implications of a book in English about her life were vague to her. Nevertheless, she cheerfully answered interminable questions and patiently repeated information obvious to any Auca but baffling to a foreigner unfamiliar with her culture. (And I suspect that she had her own reservations about the intelligence of an interrogator who required so much repetition!) The manuscript was completed in early February 1960, when Dayuma left with Rachel for their Auca home, where the rivers surge with the succulent fish, and where the forest is alive with monkeys to be had whenever the hunters decide to appear with their blowguns. There on the banks of the sparkling Tiwaeno, foreigners who plague one with questions are few. But as I write this, there is one—Dayuma's friend Rachel, who is out there now "carving" a Book intelligible to Dayuma and her people: the Holy Scriptures in their own musical Auca language.

Ethel Emily Wallis
Philadelphia
February 27, 1960

# Contents

# "I Don't Remember"

It was a still, sultry afternoon in the Ecuadorian jungle, but Dayuma's brown hands glistened with cold perspiration. Her large, wide-set black eyes glanced quickly from Rachel Saint to the microphone of a tape recorder.

"Don't be afraid—just talk," coaxed Rachel in her limited Auca vocabulary as she held the microphone toward Dayuma.

But the unusual brightness of the Indian girl's eyes and the half-nervous rubbing of her hands betrayed the inward excitement, shadowed with some apprehension, of one poised on the brink of a totally new experience. She looked again at the blue-eyed foreigner whose smile reassured her. Then, accepting the challenge, she reached daringly for the strange metal object. Rachel felt the moist coolness of Dayuma's hands as they touched hers.

"Tell me about your home in the forest before you came here," the foreigner encouraged gently.

With much repetition and some hesitation, but in a clear, strong voice, Dayuma began to review her life in the Auca forest before she had fled to the outside world and to Don Carlos Sevilla's hacienda.

With scarcely two months' study of the Auca language, Rachel did not understand every spoken word of the tragic tale. But she could read the terror and torment which flashed from Dayuma's eyes and shook her voice as she forgot the foreigner's machine and poured out her past. Dayuma was back in the jungle reliving the horrors of her childhood. And Rachel, without warning, was drawn with her into the Auca forest, bristling with cruelty.

> I was born on Fish River.
> Afterwards we lived well on Palm River.
> We saw the high hills far off clearly.
> We saw far downriver.
>
> My big brother was Wawae.
> My father was Tyaento, my mother, Akawo.
> Nampa my brother was a small child.
> Oba my sister was still younger.
> My big sister was Onaenga, my other sister, Gimari.
> My mother's relatives were many.
> My uncles were Wamoñi and Gikita.
>
> Moipa and Itaeka did not do well.
> Fleeing and hiding we came, far, far downriver.
> We went by canoe. Then we went back.
>
> When did they spear? They speared at night.
> My father escaped into the water.
> They dug a grave for him and he was caused to die.
> But he didn't die right away.
> I didn't see it. They spoke and I heard.
> My relative said, "I buried him."
>
> Moipa and Itaeka speared.
> Where did they go, did they say?
> On a small stream upriver we returned.
> We didn't see them.

We drank the water of *maeñika* fruit.
It rained, we got wet.
The jaguar growled, the monkeys called.
We climbed the trees when the jaguar came.

Then we fled.
We came at night in the moonlight.
We speared *gyaegyae* fish.

We were planting peanuts on Palm River.
The outsiders came with guns and shot.
Their dogs barked.
We went into the water, then fled on the other side....

Even after eight years of peaceful living on Don Carlos's hacienda, out of reach of the spears that had killed her father, fear and hate were still hot in the Auca girl's heart. The smoldering embers of revenge needed only to be stirred into sudden, flaming life, and in a few moments the docile day laborer of the banana fields was transformed into a wild girl of the jungle. Murder gleamed from her angry eyes as she was transported to the land of spearing and fleeing, of violence and vengeance.

"Moipa—I hate him!" Every utterance of the name of her father's murderer fanned her fury into higher flame as the chronicle gathered momentum. Rachel watched in awe as the girl's passion burst into a fire of frenzied hate. Dayuma had forgotten that the listener was a stranger to the world of spears into which she had been plunged.

The language curtain had begun to part and, through the narrow opening, Rachel caught a glimpse of the struggle still in progress a few miles east of the hacienda. She had known that the Aucas killed foreigners who came near their borders, but now she learned that intratribal feuds were fast exterminating the group itself.

Soon after Rachel's arrival at Hacienda Ila in February 1955, she had heard about Moipa, notorious killer of the forest. Dayuma, in drunken despondency, had asked Don Carlos to sell her a gun.

"Teach me how to use it," she had begged. "I want to go back to my home and kill Moipa. One with nine shots will do." And now Rachel saw that in sober hatred Dayuma still desired to avenge the death of her father, Tyaento—a duty which would normally fall to his sons.

Rachel was unprepared for the emotional upheaval caused by the recording. In the days that followed, she was to appreciate more fully the monumental achievement it had been for Dayuma. That brief narrative recounted in the Auca language was to mark the beginning of a new chapter in the history of an unsubdued Ecuadorian tribe.

❧ ❧ ❧ ❧

When Rachel had begun writing down the first Auca words from Dayuma in February, it had soon become dishearteningly apparent that the girl had all but forgotten her mother tongue. Her previous life and language lay smothering under a foreign blanket grown thick by years of Quichua Indian customs and speech.

Dayuma had purposely tried to forget her native language while living with Quichuas, who ridiculed the naked and savage Aucas. She now wore the traditional Indian dress of the region: a straight dark skirt and a loose-hanging, long-sleeved blouse. Her black hair was parted on the side and hung down over her ears, half covering the large holes in the lobes which once held chunky round plugs of balsa wood. At home in the forest her hair had been cut in bangs that extended back well beyond her ears.

But as far as Dayuma was concerned, Auca hairstyles and patterns of speech had been fast merging into oblivion when Rachel met her. "The chonta palm I planted when I arrived here, it has given its fruit five times," Dayuma told Rachel. To indicate past time, Dayuma turned down three stubby fingers in Indian fashion to account for the three years of growth necessary to produce the delicious bright orange palm fruit.

Rachel's keen disappointment was understandable, for she had searched several years to find someone who spoke the language of the dread killers of the jungle. The only available Aucas outside the tribe were living at Hacienda Ila. She *had* to learn the language here, away from the spear-marked boundaries of the hostile tribe. Don Carlos himself had invited her to come with her companion Catherine Peeke to study with the four Auca women who worked for him.

However, within a few days of their arrival at the hacienda, it had been sadly evident that three of the four women—Umi, Ominia, and Winaemi—could recall nothing of their language, even after much persistence on Rachel and Catherine's part. The struggle with them had been futile. By comparison, Rachel's efforts with Dayuma had been encouraging. During a few precious hours gleaned after the girl's long days in the fields, Rachel had patiently and laboriously struggled to dredge up from the murky recesses of the Indian girl's memory words learned as a child. After pronouncing a few words recollected with obvious effort, Dayuma would exhaust her Auca verbal supply and say with simple resignation, "*Wi mponimopa*—I don't remember," the first phrase that Rachel learned. Rachel could almost see her think. Her lips would move voicelessly over and over. But very often after trying hard Dayuma would look up at Rachel and repeat those discouraging words, "I don't remember."

The girl's delight in a determined effort to win the battle for Auca words had given Rachel heart for the tedious siege. Though ground was gained slowly at first, by the end of the first month Rachel had extracted many pages of words and phrases from her willing helper. In fact, she now had recorded phonetically more Auca words than were contained in any list available to her. In an earlier search for Auca clues, Rachel had collected several brief word lists. One was recorded by the scientist Tessman (published in 1930), and three by others who through the years had tried to establish a contact with the tribe. The most recent was a brief vocabulary Dayuma had given a missionary three years before Rachel arrived at the hacienda.

These lists, though very limited, had served the fruitful purpose of inspiring the alert Indian girl to revive the use of her own language. Rachel fondly remembers Dayuma's great surprise at her ability to look at the lists and approximate a pronunciation of the words. "I was amused when she began to look at my notes with great interest, just as if she, a completely illiterate primitive girl, could really read!"

While they were making progress, Rachel's time with Dayuma was very scarce. "Many a day," writes Rachel, "we watched the Indian girl, from whom I had hoped to learn the language, go off to the fields at dawn, machete in hand, a huge basket hanging lightly from its bark strap across her forehead. She often turned back as she took the trail, to see if she could see us at the upper windows of our new home, and usually we did not see her again until after sunset. She cleared weeds all day, then returned heavy-laden with bananas or yuca, her strong back bent low beneath the heavy load she carried. My heart would hope that she would be given time to come to our room, but often I climbed under the mosquito net at the end of the day disappointed. I had seen Dayuma only from afar!

"Occasionally the jungle rain would bring all the servants home early from the fields. Then we would wait expectantly for Dayuma to come bouncing into the room with an air of importance, sit down cross-legged on the wooden floor, and unconsciously wiggle her big bare toes as she contemplated this new turn of events which was already beginning to affect the routine pattern of her life as she had lived it for many years at Ila.

"Having no language in common with Dayuma since I had not studied Quichua, I was forced into what we had jokingly called in our courses at the Summer Institute of Linguistics, 'ye olde monolingual approach.' By motions and gestures I elicited the names for objects. The room was gloomy, so I invited Dayuma to sit near the window where I could watch her face and decipher her motions. It wasn't long before she also was using the monolingual approach with me!

"I tried sitting on the floor beside her, but I just wasn't trained for that. So I compromised and sat on a low wooden box, my notebook on my lap and pen in hand eagerly ready to write down the data that would enable me to analyze this language."

Sometimes the bright Indian girl, capturing the idea, would act out the words for Rachel by crawling like a baby or throwing herself down in a feigned fit of anger. Such antics were always accompanied by hilarious laughter, making their hours together great entertainment.

"How do you say *sun?*" Rachel asked one day, supplementing her limping language with gestures.

"*Naenki,*" responded Dayuma, then brightening, "*apaika*" and "*nimu.*" She had also offered the words for moon and stars.

Later when Rachel asked for the Auca names of the Napo and Curaray rivers, she was overjoyed when the girl went right on and named the other rivers which she had known so well as a child. She also began to recall in detail what had happened on them. The gap between the almost-forgotten past and the present was being closed by the powerful association of language.

🐍  🐍  🐍  🐍

The scattered words and sentences that came so hard at first had formed a coherent pattern crystallized on a historic magnetic tape. It was a short but moving story of why a daring Auca girl in her early teens risked her life to find something better than useless death in a cruel forest. The same valiant spirit prompted the untaught jungle girl to share her returning language with a mysterious machine and a curious stranger.

As Rachel watched Dayuma after this, her heart welled up with thanksgiving that the Lord had sent her to the Auca girl. When she looked out beyond her thatched-roofed hacienda home to the east, Rachel knew that somewhere beyond the ridge in the endless jungle lived Dayuma's people, and that someday the Lord would send her to them, too.

In the months that followed, Rachel, who had been working with Dayuma whenever opportunity afforded and analyzing the language recorded on tape and paper when she was not available, was able to fill in the details of the girl's story.

The more Rachel learned, the more convinced she became that the Aucas had earned their dreadful reputation. *Speared him dead—* the phrase recurred with striking frequency as Dayuma described the sordid end of many of her relatives. Very soon the name Moipa began to dominate the narratives. Yes, Dayuma hated him with all her heart, for this brutal killer of the forest had been responsible for many murders.

"They buried my father and he died," Dayuma had said. *Buried and died*—this phrase also began to show up in various contexts. Was it a misplaced order of words? As Rachel questioned Dayuma, she learned to her horror that the word order was true to the facts: It is Auca custom to bury alive. Because of the greatest of their fears, that of death without a burial, dying Aucas often beg to be interred before they expire. Dayuma's own father had died in his grave. Her cousin Umi, who fled the forest with her, had been a witness to the death groans which became fainter and fainter, and ended in silence.

Babies and even older children are thrown into the graves with their fathers, or left in the jungle to die alone. In cases of extreme hate and anger, victims are dug up and speared again, the avenger shrieking his wrath and railings while plunging his spear into rotting flesh. Moipa deserved such a death, Dayuma had said vindictively, but as far as she knew no one had been able to kill him.

Was there no limit to the cruelty of the savage tribe to which she had been called? Rachel was grievously appalled as she listened to Dayuma.

"The devil of the forest sucks our blood and we die," the girl reported matter-of-factly one day. "You can even see the black-and-blue spots on the bodies." This devil and other evil spirits existed for Dayuma, even on the civilized hacienda. The fears of the forest had pursued her relentlessly.

*Being cursed my father died*—ah! that was the real reason why Moipa's spears had finally succeeded after several earlier attempts. The curse of an enemy spells almost certain death for an Auca.

Stories of cannibals, foreigners who ate Auca flesh, also began to find expression in Dayuma's conversation. She described in repulsive detail the fate that had befallen Aucas who ventured beyond the safety of their own guarded borders.

"I was afraid because they said the foreigners would eat me when I ran away," she reminisced. "But I knew that Moipa would spear me if I stayed."

All foreigners were to be feared—and killed, if possible. Through the years they had ruthlessly shot down Dayuma's people with their guns and had stolen their yuca and bananas. They were a threat to the Auca food supply and to their very existence. Outsiders merited the undying hatred of her people.

As Rachel heard such verification of reported Auca hostility, her prospects of crossing the deadly borders became more remote. Even if she did learn the language from Dayuma, how could she ever set foot on Auca soil? Apart from miracles, it would be folly to consider it. But the conviction was firm that someday God would make a way to the tribe, so she plowed steadily ahead in language study. Rachel had determined to use only Auca with Dayuma, for if she learned Quichua there would be no real need for the girl to recall her own language. She often thought wistfully of all the Auca conversation going on constantly not many miles away.

Rachel sighed for the day when she would be able to put enough Auca words together to tell Dayuma about the living God. How would she begin? She had noted a word for a creator-god, but what did the term mean to the Aucas? She would need to tell Dayuma of God's Word, but how, when she had no word for "book" or "writing"?

One day a little yellow airplane flew over and dropped a bag of mail at the isolated hacienda for Rachel. In it was a letter from home—a letter written by her mother. Rachel showed Dayuma the letter and told her it was from her mother far away. She immediately responded with the words, "*bara ndiwaemonga*—mother's carving." It was a term used for gashing a tree to mark a trail or signal a message.

*God's carving*. Perhaps that would do for the expression *God's Word*. Rachel jotted the phrase down.

Dayuma was curious about the letter. How could one so far away carve a message for her daughter on a little piece of paper? What did it say to Rachel? And who brought it to Rachel's brother Nate so that he could carry it in the yellow wood-bee to Rachel? She already knew that Nate flew the wood-bee which often buzzed overhead as it crossed the sky above the hacienda. As a pilot of the Missionary Aviation Fellowship, he served isolated workers dependent upon air communication. There was no airstrip at Ila, but he often dropped a welcome package.

As the months went by, Dayuma's curiosity about the foreigner at the hacienda grew. Travelers often came and went, but this one was here to stay until she learned all the words of the Auca language. No one had ever shown so much interest in her, Dayuma thought, and no one had ever asked so many questions.

Then came the day when Dayuma began to ask Rachel questions.

"Why do you want to learn my language?" With still very limited conversational ability in Auca, Rachel was on the spot. Mustering all of her available vocabulary, she managed, "So that I can go to your people and teach them not to kill, and to live well."

A wondering look was Dayuma's eloquent reply. She had understood the words—but why would anyone want to go to the killers of the forest? She herself had no intention of returning to the place from which she had fled for her life.

"But if you go," she commented significantly, "see if my mother lives, see if my sister Gimari lives. Returning, you can tell me about them."

Dayuma was beginning to wonder again about her family over the ridge. When she first came to the hacienda, she had cried for them each night, but eventually her tears dried completely. Now Rachel's queries renewed her concern.

There were other questions brewing in the active Auca mind. "Who sent you?" was the next challenge. Using the Auca word for God, Rachel replied, "Our God, the other God, sent me to learn from you." That was a big sentence, and Rachel wondered if Dayuma understood. However, her reply was reassuring, for with a puzzled expression she said, "It must have been your God." After a pause, Dayuma then asked, "Why did you come?"

"So that I can put God's carving into your language, and teach your people what He says."

"Who taught you?"

That required a longer answer. Many people in Rachel's land knew God's carving. Her mother, and her father, and her brother who flew the wood-bee knew it. Even her grandmothers and grandfathers had known, and they taught her. Now she could read God's carving for herself.

Dayuma began to ply Rachel with more questions about her family. When would she see her mother again? How many brothers and sisters did she have? Did they all live with her mother and father?

Dayuma's answers to Rachel's questions about her jungle family were much sadder.

"Does my mother live? I don't know. Maybe she has been speared. Maybe a snake has bitten her and she has died. Maybe she died with a fever long ago.

"Does my sister Gimari live? I don't know. Do my brothers live? Maybe they have been killed by Moipa's spears."

In spite of her bitter past, Dayuma's desire to know more of the new things she was learning grew with each day's conversation. She had an unmistakable curiosity about God, but the language barrier was still frustratingly high.

"Is there dwelling-ground above the sky…? Is there dwelling-ground beneath the earth…?"

Questions, questions, and more questions. Dayuma worked hard to remember her language to teach Rachel. Then she, in turn, could give the answers which Dayuma was sure she knew.

"Why didn't you come when I first ran away?" Dayuma asked one day, after a linguistic skirmish. "I would have remembered my language fast then."

Rachel thought how much easier it would have been to learn Auca from someone who was more fluent.

Eight precious years, apparently lost.

"Why, indeed, didn't I come sooner?"

# CHAPTER TWO

# Shaken from the Nest

$W$hen Rachel had announced to friends in New Jersey one day in 1948 that she would be leaving for South America, they were thunderstruck. They had worked happily with her for years, and assumed she had settled in permanently. But Rachel had, in fact, been listening for the message that was to change the course of her life that year. It meant leaving a comfortable, happy place of Christian service and heading toward a primitive home somewhere in the tangles of Amazonian jungle.

Rachel had quickly recognized the hand that shook her cozy nest. The time had come to try her wings of faith in a distant land where countless Indian tribes were dying without God's Word.

Rachel had known that her task would involve learning an unwritten language, the key to communication with primitive people, and therefore applied for study at the Summer Institute of Linguistics. It was the first step in joining the Wycliffe Bible Translators, a mission team devoted to sharing God's Book with neglected tribespeople the world over.

ৰ্জ্ঞ ৰ্জ্ঞ ৶ৱ ৶ৱ

In the summer of 1948, Oklahoma heat pressed down on several hundred trainees for Bible translation as they struggled with sounds and syntax for eleven weeks of intensive linguistic analysis on the state university campus at Norman. At times Rachel would slip away from the books to a quiet spot by the football stadium, where under towering white clouds she could talk with the Lord who had thrust her out on this new venture. As she read His Word and waited on Him for the next step, the assurance deepened that God would lead her to an unreached tribe. She knew that there would be many opportunities to help in pioneer work already under way, but God's will for her was a tribe untouched by the Gospel. A verse from the Berkeley version of Romans reinforced the conviction: *Those who have never been told of Him shall see and those who never heard shall understand.*

After the course at the University of Oklahoma, the next step was Jungle Training Camp in southern Mexico, where Rachel learned how to live in rustic surroundings. She observed Wycliffe translators Phil and Mary Baer with the Lacandon Indians, one of the most primitive tribes of North America. It was a small tribe, and cultural barriers slowed spiritual advance into the group. Perhaps a similar challenge awaited her in the Amazon area.

In 1949, Rachel packed her duffel bags and footlockers with equipment for living far from the benefits of civilization, and was soon on her way to join Wycliffe's team in Peru. En route she stopped in Ecuador to visit her brother Nate and his wife, Marj. Nate was transporting missionaries stationed in the eastern jungle of Ecuador. He told Rachel of the tribal work in progress in the undeveloped Oriente, the sparsely populated jungle forest east of the Andes. But there was one tribe that did not welcome missionaries—the hostile Auca.

"I don't fly over them," said Nate. "I fly around them." Foreigners down through the years had tried unsuccessfully to live peaceably with the Auca tribe. A forced landing in Auca territory meant certain death, and Nate believed that his work for isolated missionaries was too vital to take the chance.

"Nate was always fearless when duty demanded facing any kind of danger," Rachel comments, "so I knew there was good reason for his cautiousness. This was the first time I had heard of the Aucas, and my heart was strangely drawn to them. If there was ever an unreached tribe, I thought, this was surely it."

In Peru, Rachel worked with the Piro Indians. Esther Matteson was already well into the language and had begun the initial stages of Bible translation. But this was not an unreached tribe, so Rachel could not settle in comfortably when there were others like the Aucas, who had heard nothing of Christ.

In another tribe of Peru—the head-hunting Shapras—two Wycliffe translators were due for furlough after several years of living in extremely rugged circumstances. Doris Cox and Loretta Anderson had learned to speak Shapra and had begun to give the Word of God to Tariri, the head-hunting chief, and others of his tribe. There had been little response to their message, however, and they were reluctant to leave their work for a much-needed rest. Finally, they decided to take their furloughs separately, if a temporary partner were available for continuing work in the tribe. Rachel willingly offered to serve as a partner first to Loretta, then to Doris.

While living with the Shapra Indians, Rachel came to love Chief Tariri and his wild people. But the chief was not yet inclined to leave the brutal practice that was his claim to tribal leadership. Decked out in his bright-colored feather headdress, Tariri was an imposing figure as he set out with his spears for a roundup in the forests of the Amazon headwaters, where northern Peru merges undramatically into Ecuador.

After two and a half years of jungle work in Peru, Rachel spent a month's vacation in Ecuador, visiting her brother Nate and his wife, Marj. She heard more about the mysterious Aucas. People on the streets and in buses were discussing the recent Auca attacks on Quichua Indians and Ecuadorians living near their borders in the jungle. Several attacks on the personnel of the Shell Oil Company base at Arajuno had hastened that company's withdrawal from the area. In Quito, Nate took his sister to visit an engineer of the company who gave more details of the ferocity of the Auca attacks. He said that he even had a feather headdress, souvenir of a raid.

"May I see the headdress?" Rachel asked.

"Certainly." The engineer promptly sent his son to fetch the trophy.

"It is exactly like Tariri's!" Rachel exclaimed in amazement. "Why, these people must be like the Shapras of Peru!"

During her days in Ecuador, a quiet, deep assurance settled on Rachel. These unapproachable Aucas were "those who have *never* been told of Him." This was the unreached tribe to which she was called. As she left Ecuador and returned to Peru, she knew that one day she would be going to the Auca tribe. "I hardly knew what to do with this new assurance," Rachel remembers. "Wycliffe was not working in Ecuador and I had no leading to leave Wycliffe. I loved this group which was as dear to me as my own family, and I couldn't think of leaving. I didn't mention the matter to anyone except a Peruvian pastor, a godly man who promised to pray for me and the tribe to which I had been called."

Rachel began to pray and plan for her future work among the Aucas. She thought of possible reasons for the Lord to have placed her for a time with the primitive Shapras. The feather headdress had been an exciting clue. Perhaps there was a cultural connection between the two tribes. If so, they might belong to the same linguistic family.

While at the Yarinacocha Jungle Base in Peru, Rachel visited with other Wycliffe workers who had been stationed for months in tribes throughout the Peruvian jungle. Among them were Catherine Peeke and Mary Sargent, who had returned from the Záparo Indians on the Pastaza River near the Ecuadorian border. Although several days by canoe from the Shapra tribe, the two young women had been Rachel's closest neighbors. As they chatted, they compared tribal notes and discussed future plans.

"Will you be returning to the Shapra tribe?" was a very natural question for Catherine and Mary to ask Rachel.

Rachel hesitated. She knew that she wouldn't return to the Shapra tribe, but how could she tell about her future plans?

"No…" she said. "My tribe is across the border."

"Across what border?"

"Across the border in Ecuador. The Aucas—"

"In Ecuador! How? Wycliffe isn't working there."

"I don't know, but I am sure that I will be working there. God will make a way...."

The conversation, which continued during the meal, was interrupted for an important announcement director Cameron Townsend wanted to make.

"I would like to read a letter which has just come from the Ecuadorian ambassador to the United States, inviting us to work among the Indian tribes of Ecuador...."

～ ～ ～ ～

Busy days of planning and packing followed as the first members of the Ecuadorian team, volunteers from among the workers in Peru, began to move northward. Though eager to begin her search for the Auca tribe, Rachel was not among the first recruits to reach Ecuador. When after a number of delays she finally arrived, she was delighted that there was fresh news concerning the tribe. She heard of an Auca girl who was living in Quito in the city home of Señor Sevilla, an Ecuadorian hacienda owner from the Oriente. Since there was no safe way to enter the tribe at this time, Rachel investigated the possibility of working with an Auca speaker to gain a knowledge of the language before the door into the tribe opened.

One afternoon when Rachel and Catherine Peeke called on Señor Sevilla, he graciously offered the services of one of his maids who spoke Auca. As Rachel wrote down the words pronounced by the girl, Catherine whispered, "This is not pure Auca. She is mixing Quichua with it." Catherine had learned Quichua while working with the Andoas Indians, and she recognized the linguistic hybridization.

In her disappointment, Rachel frankly told Sevilla that this informant would not do because she evidently did not speak the Auca language.

"That is understandable," said Sevilla, "for she is a Quichua girl who was captured by the Aucas and lived with them for many years. It is very possible that she doesn't speak pure Auca. But if you want to work with Aucas, we have four of them working on my hacienda in the Oriente."

"You do?" asked Rachel, trying to conceal her excitement.

He then told of Dayuma and Umi who had fled from their Auca home and arrived at Hacienda Ila several years before. The other two women, Wiñaemi and Omiñia, had come out later. These Aucas would be available for informant work at the hacienda.

From Señor Sevilla's city home, Rachel and Catherine went immediately to join other Wycliffe workers for an audience with President Velazco Ibarra of Ecuador, to whom Cameron Townsend was to present the members of the first group of translators. Rachel, who lacked a proper hat for the occasion, had been encouraged by Townsend to wear the bright feather headdress which Chief Tariri had affectionately presented her upon leaving his tribe. She had converted it into a fashionable headpiece by the addition of a veil. As President Ibarra cordially received the band of missionary-linguists, he displayed great curiosity when the young woman with the Indian headdress was introduced as a future Auca worker.

"What?" he said. "You mean that you expect to work with the Aucas? When I flew over them, they threw spears at the plane. No white person has ever been able to live in the Aucas' territory.... Do you really intend to go to the Auca tribe, señorita?"

"Yes," answered Rachel confidently. "I believe that God will make a way."

She was frightened later when she reflected on her boldness. "It sounded like presumption—but I was so sure, that it just tumbled out!"

Finally in February of 1955, Rachel, accompanied by Catherine Peeke, arrived downstream on the Anzu River in a Wycliffe float plane almost at the front door of Hacienda Ila. The Anzu is one of hundreds of feeders that tumble down the waning slopes of the Andes and finally succumb, many jungle miles later, to the huge and hungry Amazon. An hour by canoe downriver from Hacienda Ila, the Anzu joins the Jatunyacu to form the wide and winding Napo that cuts a muddy channel through the giant jungle and wanders on erratically across the Peruvian border. But the Napo's main reason for being, as far as the Ecuadorian settlers were concerned, was that it safely separated them from Auca territory.

Hacienda Ila, on the western side of Auca territory and protected from spears by several rows of intervening mountain ridges, had been hand carved out of virgin jungle by the industrious Sevilla family. Over a period of thirty years they had subdued the fertile area once covered by huge trees thickly draped with gigantic vines and ferns—a formidable green barrier to civilized progress.

The huge two-story thatched home of the Sevilla family was surrounded by various smaller buildings for the workers, guest houses for travelers in the jungle, a kitchen house, and even a small school for the children of the Indian laborers. Beyond the buildings lay the cultivated fields of sugar cane, bananas, yuca, and pasture for the cattle and horses. Fruit and palm trees dotted the landscape.

Living quarters at Ila reflected much of the history of the place, according to Rachel:

"The guest room the Sevilla family graciously offered us was a large one on the second floor. Like the rest of the house it was constructed of hand-hewn timbers from the forest that had been cleared to make way for the jungle mansion. From the walls several portraits looked down upon us out of their massive wood frames. There was one of Don Carlos's mother wearing a necklace of huge gold nuggets. Her gracious manner spelled old Spain. Another was of a robed and bearded priest, a mark of the Old World visible to the present day along the route of Orellana.

"The place reminded me in many ways of a medieval castle, with the turrets replaced by palm thatch, and the moat by the racing river. We were served our meals in the spacious dining room where one or more members of the Sevilla family presided. We were offered the best fare the jungle affords, adorned by Latin culinary arts and served by well-trained Quichua Indians. The conversation of our hosts and their many guests who always made Ila a stopover gave us a liberal education in the ways of the jungle."

One familiar topic was certain to be mentioned—that of Auca spearings. Don Carlos was well-qualified to lead such discussions, for he himself had been the victim of those spears. While hunting rubber on the Curaray, he had had several such encounters. His prize story was of hand-to-hand combat when the Aucas surprised him on the river. He dived into the water, swam to the other side, and climbed a fallen tree up the steep bank. One Auca who pursued him threw a spear which wounded him. The others rained spears at him, but he managed to use the same spears for counterattacking and finally drove the Aucas off. Then, burning with fever and his spear wound squirming with maggots, he walked eight days out of the forest. His faithful dog was his only companion.

The wild stories Rachel heard from Don Carlos and his venturesome visitors would have discouraged one with less conviction. Instead, Rachel seized every opportunity to study the language with Dayuma.

After one mealtime discussion of the fierce tribe, Señor Sevilla's son suggested that Rachel would probably write a book about the Aucas.

"Yes, perhaps after I have lived with them for twenty years," she replied.

"You don't expect to live among the Aucas for twenty years, do you?" he asked incredulously.

After that dialogue, Rachel wrote in her diary: "No outsider has ever lived long in their territory. It would be sheer presumption apart from God's call."

During the few precious hours Dayuma was free from her work in the fields, she faithfully taught Rachel as much of her language as she could remember. She gained confidence in the friendly foreigner who listened so sympathetically. As Rachel learned Auca, Dayuma was encouraged to recall more of it herself as a medium of detailing her early life, revived through the powerful association with her mother tongue.

In the first days of study, as Rachel extracted words by gestures and signs, it occurred to her to show Dayuma the photo album compiled during her stay with the Shapra Indians. The response was immediate. When Dayuma and the other Auca girls saw the picture of Chief Tariri with his feather headdress, they gasped and announced with assurance, "Auca!" The album was the key that unlocked the door. They pointed to the long hair, the blowguns, the monkeys, and the spears, and reacted as if they were seeing pictures of their own people back home beyond the ridge. There was one difference: Their people didn't wear clothes, while Tariri's did.

Dayuma was intrigued by Tariri and his family, and the fact that Rachel had actually lived with them. She asked Rachel to teach her the names of Tariri's wife and children and relatives. Rachel was amazed from the very first at Dayuma's keen memory. Dayuma never forgot one of those names.

As growing fluency in the language permitted, Rachel told Dayuma about the tribes in which she had lived and described some of their customs. Whenever the practices of other Indians struck a familiar note, the girl would brighten or display a startled expression. How could this newcomer know so much about the way Aucas lived? One day when Rachel mentioned that Tariri's tribe strangled babies, Dayuma became curious and wanted to know more about the Shapra custom. Soon the Auca girl was explaining to Rachel the methods of infanticide in her tribe.

During the months of patiently pulling Dayuma back into her language, Rachel saw that God had wasted no time. Every step had been perfect preparation for understanding and winning the heart of a wild girl of the forest.

As Rachel recalled with gratitude the way God had led her, she knew that He would someday complete the journey right into the heart of the forbidden land. "About a year and a half ago," she wrote in early 1955, "I flew over the eastern jungle with Nate on one of his routine runs. Perhaps twenty minutes out of his backyard at Shell Mera, he turned to me and said, 'See that ridge?'

" 'Just beyond that ridge is where your Aucas live,' he volunteered.

"A way of reaching the Aucas then seemed just as vague as the green nothingness that was lost on the horizon. But the Lord's call and the Lord's promises seemed just as solid as the jungle ridge, the visible boundary between the Aucas' territory and the rest of the jungle. The real boundary was marked, however, by years of killing which had repulsed all foreigners.

"Now I am closer to Aucaland. As I gaze out of the window of the hacienda to which the Lord has brought me, I am close to the land of the Aucas, although I cannot see it. What I see is a ridge, rising from the swift Anzu River to the east, in an ever-changing tapestry of jungle verdure, varied with tropical sun or dark rainstorms. The ridge is ever there, just as solid as faith's promises, the first thing I see in the morning, and the last as the lingering sun sets.

"As I look off across the ridge to Aucaland, with perhaps not one but several groups of people living there without God and without hope, I wonder myself just how the Lord will make the way. Somehow, I feel that when He does, it will be a safe one, for He doeth all things well."

# CHAPTER THREE

# "With My Father in the Forest"

Sometimes on dark jungle evenings after Rachel had given up hope of seeing Dayuma that day, she would hear the muffled thumping of bare feet on the stairs. Overtones of giggles and whispers announced the arrival of Dayuma and her companions for a late visit. The women would chatter and chuckle around the smoky kerosene lamp. Occasionally, they would oblige with a rhythmic nasal chant from the forest. In Auca falsetto they would sing the same syllables over and over—refrains from ancestral tunes too ingrained to be forgotten.

In such a mood, Dayuma would be inspired to recount the happy hours of her childhood when her relatives would gather for whole nights of singing and dancing.

❧   ❧   ❧   ❧

For days before a big party the jungle would ring with shouts of glee as the children joined in the excitement of the coming event. On tall poles outside the thatched huts were fastened the backbones of river fish which attracted clouds of beautiful butterflies. They danced in the bright sunshine as if anticipating the celebration.

Under the fluttering butterfly clouds, the men laughed heartily as they wove brilliant headdresses of red and yellow toucan feathers to be worn at the dance. Some crowns were completed with several tall, soft white feathers of the heron or scissorshawk placed majestically at the back. Bright-colored feathers hung loosely down from the stand of white plumes. Upper-arm bands of colored and white feathers, and chest ornaments made of animal teeth and bones completed the costume. Red achiote paint from jungle seed smeared on bare brown bodies was the finishing touch which announced it was dance time.

The children wished they could have a party every night and climb trees and play all day. But unfortunately, there was hard work for every little Auca. Fast-growing jungle weeds had to be cleared for planting yuca and bananas, and there was always firewood to be chopped. Dayuma's cousin Umi was her faithful accomplice in jungle escapades. They would often get spanked with nettles by Uncle Gikita or big brother Wawae for not doing their chores. How those nettles did sting! But the punishment was soon forgotten, and off they went for another romp in the forest.

There were so many exciting places to play, especially the big forbidden landslide. "You'll die!" warned the parents. But Auca children were seldom afraid of anything. They loved to climb high up the slope, clinging to jungle vines, then come whooping and yelling down the steep landslide. After a big rain it was especially treacherous, but that was when it was the most fun for Dayuma. One day just after they had slithered down the hillside, there was an avalanche of earth large enough to have buried them. That time Dayuma's father, Tyaento, brushed the stinging nettles over their bare bodies, raising huge welts.

One of the greatest joys of the forest was to splash and play with the alligators on Fish River when the sun was hot. It was great fun to tease the sluggish animals sleeping lazily on mahogany logs by the water. The children punched and poked them with sticks to make them move. Finally the creatures would tire of the torment and plop down into the water.

Tyaento would often take the children to a deep place in the river where they could dive and stay under the water a long time. One of their games was to put huge stones on their shoulders or weigh themselves down with stones on their chests so they would sink. The one who could stay on the bottom the longest was the champion.

At home there were many things for children to learn. Young boys had to be taught how to spear. The men would take their sons with their spears to a field of banana trees. For days the spear training would continue, until the young boys could hit the banana-tree target accurately and bring the "enemy" down.

Boys had to learn to spear fish and blowgun monkeys and birds. Tyaento would take his sons into the forest to teach them, and Dayuma, as her father's favorite, would often accompany them. Those trips were the happiest days of her life.

Dayuma's memories of her mother, Akawo, were not so pleasant. She had never forgotten Akawo's threat when she was still very small and too young to sense the anxiety when Tyaento was several days overdue in returning from the forest. Akawo had seen the spears strike many times in her own family, and she dreaded the day when she would be left alone to provide yuca and meat for hungry children. In her fear she said to Dayuma, "If your father doesn't come back tomorrow, I will kill you. Choked with a vine around your neck, you will die. Then I will bury you in a rotten tree trunk."

*Why does my mother talk like that?* wondered little Dayuma. *Why will she kill me if my father doesn't return?*

Akawo's apprehension had been mounting for seven days. Tyaento had gone upriver to hunt, and it was upriver that Moipa had gone to live, promising that someday he would spear his relative Tyaento, with whom he had quarreled.

Surely by this time Tyaento's body, pierced by chonta spears, lay unburied in the forest. Now who would bring home meat for so many hungry mouths? A partial solution lay in reducing the number to be fed. Dayuma was the youngest—a skinny little Auca who probably wouldn't live anyway. She often suffered from high fevers, and chances for survival seemed very slim.

In her hammock that night, Dayuma looked up at the steady, luminous stars keeping vigil over the jungle forest. She kept wondering about her mother's firm words as she had threatened, "I will kill you tomorrow...."

*Will my father come tomorrow? Will he come...?* Tormented by the prospect of being choked by a strong jungle vine tied firmly around her thin neck, the child sobbed softly in her hammock. Finally, weary with fear and wondering, the tired Indian girl fell asleep.

Nearby, the Fish River, tumbling down from the melting snows of the Andes, raced eagerly on toward the Curaray. Only the ceaseless singing of the water or the occasional howl of a monkey broke the silence of the dark forest.

Akawo could not sleep. From her hammock she stirred the embers of the dying fire and planned for the future. After choking Dayuma, should she take the other children and flee? Moipa was sure to come and kill her and them. He often killed women and children, and he would not be satisfied with Tyaento's death. But where should she flee to be safe from Moipa's spears?

When Dayuma awoke, the first rays of light were filtering through small, scattered peepholes in the dense green wall of palm and giant fern. Sleep had revitalized the thin body. Her keen mind was instantly wide awake.

*If my father doesn't come today, she will kill me!* Then, quick as a flash of jungle lightning, she said to herself, *She won't choke me. I'll run away. I will hurry up and run fast. I will flee to the bramble patch—she won't get me there. If my father dies, I will live as an orphan, I will live all alone. I will take a small pot and cook yuca and eat alone. Then I will live to grow up!*

The little Auca's will to survive was strong, and plans for escape were being firmly plotted in her young mind. She sprang out of the hammock and looked around with the alertness of a canny animal of the forest. Akawo was muttering as she poked the fire and plunked a big clay pot on to boil. Dayuma glanced around the thatched hut and made a quick inventory of its scant equipment. She saw a small clay pot in the corner beside her mother's hammock. *That one will do,* she thought. And she looked again to see if the long fire stick was in its place above the fire. Yes, there it was wrapped in a leaf—she would take that to make her fire. She had twirled the stick before when she went with her father into the forest, and she could do it again.

Though very young, Dayuma had heard of many Auca children thrown out in the forest for the animals to eat, or choked with vines, or buried alive. She had heard so much that she knew her mother was not just talking. Many were the times she had fallen asleep in her hammock as her mother and father and grandfather reviewed tribal spearings and fleeings and infant killings.

There was the tale of the woman who had two children, one big enough to play and the other a small baby. When the foreigners came—one of the many groups of outsiders who periodically invaded Auca territory—the woman fled. In the jungle the baby cried a lot. "Why should I keep this baby? He cries so much," said the mother. And she threw it away. "In the jungle the baby died alone" was the matter-of-fact conclusion of the tale.

There was also Natani, Kiwa's wife, who was carrying her baby up a hill by the Tiwaeno River. She left her baby there in the jungle, and the baby died. Sometime later Natani's father said to her, "Where is your child? I haven't seen her lately." But Natani didn't answer, and her father wondered about it. Then one day another child was born, a very tiny baby. "Watch out. Don't you throw this one away," cautioned her father. And that one grew up.

Then there was Aka, one of Moipa's wives, who threw a child away. When Moipa came home from spearing, he said, "Where is my child?"

Aka didn't answer. Then her old mother spoke up,

"The baby cried and cried when we went to the jungle. We dug in the ground and buried her."

"Why did you do that?" asked Moipa. "That wasn't good."

"She threw this one away for no good reason," said the old mother. "Later she will have another one."

"Well, then, don't act like that again," said Moipa.

In her childish bewilderment, Dayuma didn't know which would be worse—to be choked to death or to be buried alive. What would it feel like to be thrown into a hole and have the dirt heaped on you until you died? She remembered the child who was born without a foot. "How will he get about without his foot?" asked the mother. Then she dug a hole, buried the baby, and it died. The story could be repeated for many Auca infants.

All morning Dayuma watched her mother as the jungle sun rose higher in the sky. She did not turn her back on her mother, but observed her every move. How happy she was when her mother sent her to the stream for a small pot of water! There at the water's edge, she looked again at the path leading off into the jungle and decided that she would flee downriver.

*Perhaps I could run away. I could live with the deer in the jungle and eat palm nuts,* she thought.

"If your father doesn't come by this afternoon, yes, I will kill you," Dayuma's mother reminded her when she returned with the water.

Dayuma watched the sun anxiously. Soon it would be noon.

Sometime before noon, her father came home. Dayuma was very happy. "Now my father has not died after all. My father is alive!" she said joyfully.

In the afternoon when Tyaento had put his spear away and had his banana drink, he went down to the water's edge. A happy daughter followed him. When they were alone, Dayuma said, "Father, Mother said she was going to kill me. 'If your father doesn't come by this afternoon, yes, I will kill you,' she said. And I cried and cried."

"But I am alive," said Tyaento comfortingly. "Now you will grow up with me. Then when you are grown up I will say, 'No, don't do things for your mother. You work for me.' "

But for a long time Dayuma didn't grow. Monkey meat and the banana drink which ordinarily made children plump had no effect on the ailing little Auca. This made her mother angry. Later she grew and became fat. Her father was very happy. "Now my child has become big," he said. Then her mother said, "Now you make things. You are no longer sick with a fever. Who is going to clear the weeds in my banana patch and in my yuca patch?"

Dayuma was very angry. "When I was a little child, I did lots for you," she said, "but you were angry with me. You were going to kill me. Now I will not work for you. I will work for my father, yes, but I won't work for you."

However, several years later when her sister Gimari was born, Dayuma did help her mother, who was sick and could not care for the baby. Dayuma would sling the infant in a bark cloth on her back and bound off into the forest to play in her favorite spots. Baby Gimari loved riding on her big sister's back where she jiggled and jogged up and down as her lively sister, not daunted by her constant companion, pursued her fun.

Dayuma's childhood pulsed with thrilling adventures in the forest, and fun with brothers and sisters and other playmates. It was only when the horrible spears struck, or when overpowering storms threatened to destroy the forest and all those living in it, that the brightness of life was overshadowed by sorrow.

One hot, humid day, Dayuma's younger sister Onaenga went to the river to fish. Dayuma stayed home with the younger children, Nampa and Gimari. Her father and older brother Wawae had gone farther downriver to spear fish.

The family had recently moved to a new settlement still surrounded by tall trees. An epidemic had weakened the men soon afterward, and they were unable to clear the heavy forest, which was dangerously close if there were jungle storms.

Dayuma watched as the clouds darkened and began to drop heavy rain. Just as Onaenga returned from fishing, the wind burst through the clearing, howling angrily and whipping the tops of the trees. It whirled down and snatched vines and pieces of the thatched roofs, tossing them crazily into the torrents of rain now flooding the ground. Lightning gashed the black sky, followed by blasts of thunder which rocked the forest.

Suddenly, large trees were ripped up by the roots, and others toppled over as if they had been chopped. The huts upon which they fell were demolished.

Onaenga grabbed little Gimari as Dayuma took their baby brother Nampa in her arms and started running. She watched the giant trees to see which way they would fall, then threw Nampa ahead of her, out of their path.

"If I die, I die," Dayuma said, "but Nampa will be saved. Get out of the way quick!" she called to the others, but they couldn't hear in the roar of the storm. Onaenga was killed, but somehow Gimari survived.

Akawo was kept from running fast by pain in her foot from a ray fish sting. She was struggling up one of the paths leading away from the hut when a big tree thundered down in front of her. Had she been running, the tree would have crushed her. Dayuma, who thought her mother had been killed, was near enough to call, "Mother, Mother, were you killed?"

"Oo, oo—" came a faint answer. And there was her mother, right in the bramble patch!

🐌 🐌 🐌 🐌

As Rachel listened, Dayuma exclaimed, "How happy I was to hear my mother's voice!"

Happy to hear the voice which had threatened to choke her a few years before...

# CHAPTER FOUR

# "My Grandfather Told Me"

As a child, Dayuma had wanted to know about God. Akawo would tell her all she knew, which wasn't much. She told her that long ago God created all the animals, and all the rivers, and all the Aucas.

Turning to Tyaento, Dayuma asked, "Father, where does God live now?"

"I don't know where He lives," Tyaento answered. "But He won't become old and die. A long, long, long time He will live."

Then he sent Dayuma to old Grandfather Karae, who knew much more. The old man informed her that not only did God create all the animals, but that when He created the ugly big black tapir, the Aucas were very much afraid of it. But God just laughed at them. Along with his stories of creation, old Karae would sing a song, "God created, God created everything," over and over again. There were several verses telling how He created first man, then animals.

In the beginning God created three Auca men and three women. When the women became pregnant, the men sharpened bamboo to make knives so that they could perform Caesarean deliveries. Although the babies survived birth, the women all died soon afterward.

Later when one of the girls grew up and was going to give birth, her husband sadly went out into the forest to sharpen the bamboo. Meanwhile, a rat appeared in the form of an Auca and told the woman how to massage to help her child to be born. He told her how to pull a cord out of the hammock to make a hole through which the child could drop. He further instructed her to put a piece of bark across the hammock to which she could cling when her pains were severe. The rat had stationed his children to watch for the return of the Auca man. As the warning was given, the rat and his children ran away. When the man arrived, the child was already born, and the mother hadn't died. He was amazed and delighted. And because of the rat's instruction, the women lived, and their children were brought up on mothers' milk.

After God had finished creating man and animals, He went up to the skies, never to return.

"How sad," thought Dayuma as a child, "that God would never come to earth again."

She often wondered what would happen to her after she died. She asked her father, "Having died, what will become of me?"

"Your body, having died, will rot," he answered.

"Then what?"

"Then your skeleton will decay."

"Then what?"

"I don't know. Ask your grandfather. He will know."

Then Dayuma asked Grandfather Karae the same question, and he, as usual, knew more than anyone else. He knew much about life after death.

"When your body rots," he said, "your soul will live."

"Where will I live?"

"You will go high up in the sky."

"Where is the trail?"

"It is just a very small trail. It goes up there on the plateau. Then it goes down and down. There is just one trail; there is no other. There is only one trail by which you may go. Having arrived over there, you will see a huge worm, as large as a full-grown tree. All who die go along that trail. If one doesn't return, he will go fast over the top of the worm and up into the sky. But if he is afraid, he will return here, and then become a termite. Here where they buried you, up in the crossbeam of your house, you will become a termite."

"Then what will happen to me, Grandfather, if I become a termite?"

"I don't know. That is the end. You become a termite."

"But I don't *want* to become a termite, Grandfather!" Turn into an insect after she died? The thought troubled the child as she continued to ply him with questions.

"Then what happens to the ones that go high up in the sky?"

"There high up in the sky it is like the top of a hill. There they will eat fruit. All of those who die and go there, in the same way they will eat fruit, high up in the sky. Then they will live."

"Then will they die again, Grandfather?"

"Yes, they will die again. In the same way, others will kill them."

"Will they kill the soul?"

"Yes, they will kill the soul."

"What will they eat, high up in the sky?"

"Well, if they have just been speared, they will eat chonta palm nuts. If they have been killed by a poisonous snakebite, they will eat yuca. If they die from fever, they will also eat yuca and peanuts."

Grandfather knew a great deal about what would happen to her after she died, but there was much more that Dayuma wanted to know. At night around the fire she would ask Grandfather to tell her more about God and the things one couldn't see. But not even Grandfather could answer all her questions.

# CHAPTER FIVE

# Outsiders

As a very small child, Dayuma had noticed a long scar on Grandfather Karae's bare body. It stretched all the way across his abdomen.

"How did you get hurt, Grandfather?" Dayuma asked one day, looking at the scar. Then he told her of the attack of outsiders when he barely escaped with his life.

It happened one day as he and some of the other relatives were out in the forest hunting monkeys. All of a sudden, he told her, "the foreigners came secretly and shot their guns." Karae's daughter was killed. As her mother, for whom Dayuma was named, picked up the body, she was killed. Dayuma's father, Tyaento, was slightly wounded, but a bullet tore across Grandfather Karae's abdomen, making a big hole. The wound was so deep that the liver was exposed, and he bled a great deal. It looked for a time as if he wouldn't live, but he recovered slowly.

The long scar was a perpetual reminder of the danger from the outside world. Aucas had to learn to watch and be wary of strangers, and to defend themselves from attack.

Her father's grandmother Wagingamo was down at the stream one day with several relatives beating out *barbasco* roots to extract poison for fishing. Strangers suddenly appeared over the hill and began shooting at the Aucas. Wagingamo's son-in-law was killed, and she and two small children were captured. As they were being hustled along the trail, they came to a steep hill. Wagingamo said to her oldest grandchild, "This is where we will flee from the outsiders. They don't understand our language."

Then Wagingamo turned on the trail and said in Auca to one of the foreigners behind her, "What is that I see over there? Look!" She pointed to a distant ridge. When he turned, she quickly pushed him over the side of the hill, gun and all. By the time he had scrambled up the hill, Wagingamo and the two children were out of sight.

Among the Aucas themselves there were differing opinions regarding those who lived outside their borders. These outsiders were never welcome within their territory. Some said there were no good outsiders, that all non-Aucas were very bad. Others believed, because of firsthand experiences, that outsiders living downriver on the Curaray were exceedingly bad, but that those living downriver on the Napo were fairly good. Around the fires at night the discussions continued loud and long, and incidents were cited to strengthen each position, either pro or con.

To the Aucas all outsiders were foreigners, whether they were of the extensive Quichua tribe surrounding Auca territory, or whether they spoke the language of the Spanish conquerors or of other white men. The Aucas made no distinction between the groups that composed the outside world.

From time to time outsiders made successful raids and captured Aucas. Some never returned, but a number escaped and were reunited with their families. Karae told the story of one captive who had lived for years with strangers on the other side of the Napo. But one night she escaped. "Downriver where the Napo was very big, swimming she crossed the river," Karae said.

When she arrived at her former home, however, her own relatives didn't understand her, for she spoke with a strange accent. "Why don't you speak well?" they inquired. After a while she sounded again like an Auca.

Still another group of outsiders were known to kill Aucas and cook them with salt. Since salt is not native to Auca diet, this was proof to them that the cannibals were not of their tribe. Miipu, who had been captured by the cannibals, witnessed the killing and cooking of one of his own relatives, Awaenga, who had also been captured with his wife and their small child. The wife escaped, but Awaenga was tied to a tree and shot. Then when he was "a little bit rotten," his captors hacked up the body and threw it into a pot with salt. Miipu was forced to eat his relative's flesh, much to the delight of the cannibals. He escaped, went back to his people, and reported, "There you will not live well. They are not good foreigners."

Little wonder that through the years the tribe feared they would fall into the hands of those who ate Auca flesh. In making contacts with any outsiders, this hazard had to be considered.

Because the Aucas spoke no language in common with outside dwellers they constantly misunderstood and clashed with all who approached them, regardless of the foreigners' motives.

Grandfather had a great store of tales about the Wiñatarae, a group of Aucas living in a different area of the jungle. They were very large and made long spears. They also made huge pots, two or three feet high, which when turned upside down were good hiding places. Once during an attack, some of them hid under their pots and were not killed.

As a child, Dayuma heard the odd speech of the Wiñatarae. Her father could understand them, but she could not follow their conversation.

Earlier, in her grandfather's day, a group of the Wiñatarae had silently settled themselves in an empty Auca hut near the banana and yuca fields of their neighbors and were helping themselves to a rich supply of food. Two Auca heroes, Tipayae and Ima, on discovering their big thatched hut and land appropriated by the thieves, planned to wipe them out.

They built themselves a palm-thatched shelter, high above the enemy in one of the largest trees of the forest and hidden from sight in the crotch of the tree. They even cooked in a small clay pot over a fire made by friction sticks. There they lived for more than a month. Every time they went down for water or food, they would spear one or two Wiñatarae. After killing a few, they would circle way around, "just like jaguars," and hide once again in the tree. Thus they killed many of the Wiñatarae, the siege continuing until their spear supply was exhausted.

One of Grandfather's favorite stories was of a very short Auca man who had a narrow escape from an outsider. He was so anxious to get his peanuts down from the rafters of his hut when the outsiders came, that he didn't have time to run away into the forest. So he ducked under a canoe which was turned upside down. The outsiders came, and one of them sat near the canoe. The short man quickly reached out from under the canoe, grabbed a club, and gave the intruder a fatal blow on the head.

"For one year, and for two years, the outsiders didn't come back to the Aucas' huts," laughed Grandfather as he finished the tale.

The approach of outsiders was usually heralded by the barking of their dogs—a warning for the Aucas to be on guard. An Auca man who had never before seen the foreign animal, killed one when it wandered into his clearing. Some of the children listening to Grandfather had never seen dogs either, but they laughed anyway as he told the story.

Moipa and his brother Itaeka, who had become part of Karae's family after their parents were speared, would discuss the problem of outsiders with Tyaento. "Why don't we make friends with foreigners?" Tyaento often asked Moipa. But Moipa had no desire for peaceful contacts with any of them. He hated them all. As a young man he began to make raids on those living on Auca borders. Tyaento was of another persuasion. He reasoned that if the hostility continued, the outsiders would eventually gather their forces, come in, and take all the Auca territory.

The years only increased Moipa's hatred of outsiders—and of several people living in his own land.

# CHAPTER SIX

# Moipa

"Long, long before you were born," old Grandfather Karae once told Dayuma, "there were many of us. Then our people began spearing among themselves. They killed and killed until there were only a few left. Finally, someone said, 'Now we have killed enough. Why do we kill so much?'" Others agreed, and for a long time the tribe lived without many spearings.

However, within Dayuma's own family group, occasional murders left an imprint of terror on the young child's mind. While still living in Tyaento's home, Moipa and Itaeka killed the father of little Gomoki, Dayuma's relative and playmate, who with her parents also lived in the same group. It was the first spearing that Dayuma had witnessed. She still remembered it with horror:

"Very early in the morning, Moipa and Itaeka spear-killed. 'Why do they have Gomoki's father in the middle of the hammock with one of them on either side of him? Why are they doing that?' I was there in the hut watching. Being a child, I was playing. Then I saw one of them blink his eyes. 'Why is he doing that? Why is he blinking his eyes?' Then, quick as a flash, they grabbed Gomoki's father. 'Hurry! Spear him!'

"Moipa grabbed a spear. Then I ran away. To the vines and the underbrush we children fled—there were several of us—and I was terribly frightened. After they speared Gomoki's father, my father came looking for us and called, 'Where did you go? They have killed our relatives. Now you can come back.' Moipa had killed Gomoki's father and her mother and her little sister. I saw her father lying there looking alive. He didn't die fast; he died after a long while. When they spear in the throat, one dies fast, but he didn't die fast. I was very much afraid. My mother was there, but she didn't speak.

"Gomoki was very little then, when they speared her father. Then my father took her and she grew up with us. She was an orphan. Three little children my father took at that time."

Not satisfied with this cruelty, Moipa returned later and speared the three-year-old daughter of the same family. Then he took Gomoki and Aepi, a young captured Quichua girl who was living with Dayuma's family, and attempted to torture them to death. He tied their wrists together and, according to Dayuma, "threw them in the deep water. What could they do in the water like that? They were tied up tight. They went down, then they bobbed up again. Then they breathed and went down in the water again. Then Moipa threw them out of the water, then he threw them in again. My father found them there and helped get them out of the water. I went there, but Moipa had gone. He was nowhere to be found. I went, and the two of them were about to die. Then I pushed their stomachs, which were huge. Then they threw up all the water.

"I was just small then. But they got better. Then my father said to Gomoki and Aepi, 'Don't you two stay in the hut or they will kill you. Both of you follow me.' So they went everywhere with my father, and they both lived to grow up. If my father hadn't found them in the deep water, they would have died."

Through the years, Tyaento rescued other children orphaned by spearings and raised them as his own.

At that time the Aucas lived in large oval thatched huts. Dayuma's family group occupied ten such huts, each containing many people. In one, for example, there were eleven men with all their wives and children. Altogether there were several hundred in the related group living on or near the Tiwaeno River.

Dayuma's permanent front teeth were just growing in when her relatives started to kill one another. There was a nightmare of chain-reaction spearing. Within a few days the Aucas living in the ten large huts were reduced to a handful of survivors, who occupied only four small huts.

Moipa and his brother Itaeka were comparatively inexperienced spearers when the big feud began. The lull in intratribal killing was brutally broken. Aentyaeri, Dayuma's relative who initiated the mass spearing, had observed Moipa's budding ability as a killer and knew that his chance of wiping out his enemies would be multiplied with Moipa's help. When the slaughter ended, Moipa had become an experienced killer and vigorously perpetuated the tradition of spearing within the tribe and on its borders.

Eventually, Moipa and Itaeka withdrew from Tyaento's home. But two other relatives, Kimo and Dabu, brothers whose parents had been speared, stayed on in Dayuma's family.

When Dayuma was still a small girl, her people found that large numbers of outsiders were pressing close to their borders, and some had even crossed the line. Moipa had investigated this encroachment and discovered "a big house where many foreigners slept." He had noticed the foreign wood-bee buzzing overhead and dropping things on the edge of his land. Moipa was highly displeased with these activities.

Unknown to the Aucas, the Shell Oil Company had, by 1940, established a base on the Arajuno River, serviced from the larger base of Shell Mera at the foot of the Andes. Moipa resisted the approach of these foreigners who were nosing into his territory, and speared six of them before disappearing into the forest.

One day he saw a number of men walking on a small trail. He watched them take a larger trail to the river.

"I am going to kill those people," he said. "Why do they come here?"

With the help of his brother Itaeka, he followed the foreigners' trail to the big house. There they speared several of them before being bombarded by bullets. Moipa narrowly escaped death when the bullets grazed him.

"They just couldn't kill Moipa!" exclaimed the other Aucas.

When Moipa returned home, he began to gather full forces for an attack which would wipe the foreigners out. He threatened Dayuma's father and her brother Wawae if they refused to go. They went along, although Tyaento was reluctant. When the party arrived at the foreigners' camp, however, there were no people in sight. But they plundered the settlement, overturning, destroying, and throwing away most of the equipment. Barrels and bags of rice and flour were dumped. "What could this possibly be?" they asked one another as they tasted something very sweet. It was sugar—a food of which the Aucas had no knowledge or appreciation. "This is no good," they decided, and threw it away.

Then they took the foreigners' bed clothes. "Now we will sleep covered," said those who had observed how the invaders slept. But after covering themselves with the strange bed clothes, they said, "They stink!" and threw them away also. They took home some of the foreigners' yuca for their wives to see. Secretly at night the wives added it to their own prepared yuca. Then in the morning when the men had their yuca drink, they said, "What might this be? It stinks!" So they threw it all out and laughed and laughed.

Later Moipa observed the foreigners' wood-bee buzzing over the Curaray where it would drop bundles in a certain spot. He followed the air trail and discovered a lone foreigner chopping down the trees and making a camp.

The distant outpost was manned by a Shell Company employee who was preparing the way for an exploration team to follow. The plane dropped food, clothes, and other supplies at the isolated spot.

Moipa went to Tyaento's place and tried to enlist a raiding party to halt the advance of the foreigners in the area. Dayuma's brother Wawae listened with interest. He was a lazy fellow who tried to avoid work as much as possible. He begged *chambira* palm fiber from other relatives instead of cutting and preparing his own material for weaving hammocks and fishing nets. Wawae did enjoy hunting, however, and it was he who often brought Dayuma her favorite monkey meat.

The idea of a raid with Moipa appealed to Wawae, and he went with him to the Curaray. There they found the solitary foreigner strumming a guitar. They speared him and stole his clothes, which

Moipa and Wawae wore home. They never removed them, until finally the clothes rotted away and dropped off.

Each time Moipa returned from attacking the foreigners, it was evident that Tyaento disapproved of his action.

"Moipa does not do well," he would say morosely.

Tyaento and Moipa differed on other issues, too. Moipa was taking one wife after another, and had already speared one who was thin and did not please him. Tyaento argued that if this continued, there would be no women left for the younger men to marry. The friction between the two men grew steadily.

Others of the tribe had counts against Moipa, too, and he knew that someday his luck would run out and he would be speared. In preparation for that day, the chief killer had selected a successor, young Naenkiwi, whom he had trained to spear his enemies and resist further attempts of foreigners to take Auca territory.

Dayuma's concern for her father's safety increased with the years. As her apprehension grew, she talked with her father of the possibility of his being killed by Moipa. What should she do then? Should she stay and be killed by his spears that were certain to fall on other members of the family, or should she flee outside to the foreigners and take her chances? Tyaento considered the foreigners a safer risk.

Dayuma saw a heaviness clinging to Tyaento one evening when he returned from hunting. He had had little success. The monkeys he hit had refused to die.

"I am cursed," he said darkly. "Moipa will kill me soon."

Not long afterward Tyaento, in need of yuca for the large family, set off through the forest for the yuca patch. Old Karae went along, and Gimari and cousin Umi. Dabu joined the party as they started on the overnight trip.

They slept under a big felled *giminiwae* tree, the base of which had several compartments formed by wall-like roots fanning out in all directions and providing convenient sheltered nooks.

Stealthily, Moipa had followed the little group. He waited until they had fallen asleep before attacking. He fatally wounded Karae while the others escaped. Tyaento was speared in the knee.

Someone ran back through the forest to warn the others who had stayed home. Dayuma fled at the first shout of danger. Her brother Nampa said to Akawo, "Quick, Mother, let's flee." She snatched baby Oba and ran out into the night.

Shortly, Moipa arrived at the big hut and started spearing. An old uncle who had not been able to flee was his first victim. Moipa drove his spears into the old man who cried out, "I fed you, I brought you meat—when you were young I killed animals in the forest and brought them for you. Why do you kill us now?"

"Oh, just because—" yelled Moipa. "And I'll kill all the foreigners, and kill all of you off, and I alone will live!"

In the shuffle, several small children had been left behind. Moipa hacked Dayuma's little sister Nimu to pieces with his machete. He wished that more of Tyaento's children had been within reach.

But by dawn Dayuma, along with several companions and Aepi—who had taught Dayuma some Quichua words against this day—were deep in the forest, heading for the Curaray.

# CHAPTER SEVEN

# Beyond Reach of Spears

From the day Dayuma disappeared down-river flanked by dark forest, her mother, Akawo, had watched for her return.

*She is very young,* thought Akawo. *She will hide in the forest. When she is sure Moipa has gone to his hut, she will return.*

But Akawo was wrong. Dayuma was already several days down the Curaray. Although in her early teens, she was an intrepid pioneer, the valiant leader of the venture. Her companions wanted to turn back as they began their hasty departure down the Curaray, but Dayuma spurred them on. She poled the canoe downriver in spite of hunger and driving jungle rains. Dayuma was determined that nothing would turn her from her purpose.

But suddenly, at a bend in the river, she saw a relative with her baby on her back. She had cut through the forest and overtaken them. She poured out details of the raid which Dayuma had anticipated. Her mother? She did not know whether Akawo was dead or alive. That was too much for Dayuma. She must know about her mother.

Turning the party back, she poled upriver for five days, looking all the way for signs of the escaping relatives. Eventually her search was rewarded. There on a beach was the familiar print of her mother's foot.

"My mother is alive! She lives!"

Dayuma's voice trembled with joy as she followed the footprints from the beach to the forest, then through the trail until she found her mother.

"Mother, come with us," she begged immediately. "Come with us to the foreigners' houses. If you stay here, you will surely be speared."

But Akawo preferred death in the forest to fear of the unknown beyond, and refused to go. So once again Dayuma set out for the Curaray, accompanied now by her cousin Umi and Aepi.

Umi had been with Tyaento when he was speared. As they traveled downriver, she gave Dayuma the details of her father's death. After Moipa's barbed spear had pierced his knee, Tyaento knew that he would die. He hid in the forest along with other survivors, and was without food and burning with fever. He then begged his relatives to bury him alive.

They dug his grave and put Tyaento in it. Then after covering him over with bamboo slats, they began to fill the hole with earth as Tyaento groaned in pain. The moans became fainter and fainter.

"In the morning we heard nothing," concluded Umi. "I saw it. Your father is dead."

Dayuma, weeping bitterly, continued her way down the Curaray, poling the canoe with strong, determined strokes. They came to a huge settlement of foreigners who gathered around them and stared. The three girls quickly retreated and hid in the bushes beside the river. But the foreigners treated them kindly, giving them food and clothing. It was the first time Dayuma and Umi had experienced the feel of clothing on their skin, although Aepi had worn clothes and explained the foreign custom to them.

The settlement was an obsolete rubber-hunting camp manned by Quichua Indians stationed on the Curaray for their patrón, Señor Sevilla, who lived on an hacienda far to the west on the Anzu River.

Señor Sevilla had ordered that any Aucas who came out on the Curaray should be treated kindly and brought to him at Hacienda Ila. Word was therefore sent ahead to Sevilla, and after a stay of two months on the Curaray, the three girls found themselves being taken to Camp Arajuno, en route to the hacienda. When they had crossed the Oglán River, Señor Sevilla himself met the girls, bringing with him new clothes to replace the ones given them earlier. Then they continued their jounrey to Camp Arajuno.

Dayuma suddenly found herself in a new world. Someone offered her a cigarette. Tobacco was unknown in the Auca forest, and she hated the smell of it.

Her greatest shock came without warning as she found herself suddenly face-to-face with a big black animal displaying huge teeth. It was a beast of terrifying proportions, which could surely eat her alive with such monstrous teeth! She had learned to cope with jaguars and boas, but never had she seen or heard of a horse.

Finally, Dayuma, Aepi, and Umi arrived at the hacienda. There were advantages in this outside world, which Dayuma was quick to see. They were given food and clothing, and the threat of Moipa's spears seemed far, far away. There was a price to pay for safety though. The wild, unbound life of the forest was replaced by a long, daily round of chores: planting yuca, gathering bananas, pounding the hulls from rice, or harvesting sugarcane. There were heavy loads of firewood to carry for the hacienda kitchen. The kitchen furnished dozens of meals a day to the family of the patrón, his guests, and the large corps of field laborers.

Dayuma did not mind the hard work, for she was young and strong, but she did miss the trips into the forest and carefree larks down jungle rapids. When the girls were hungry for monkey meat, Señor Sevilla would send someone to hunt for them, and when time allowed, there were occasional swims in the Anzu.

Still, the price of freedom sometimes seemed too great to Dayuma. Three times she and her companions, overcome with homesickness, tried to leave. But each time they were brought back and set to work at their treadmill of hacienda chores.

〰 〰 〰 〰

Back in the forest, Akawo watched for Dayuma's return. The days and weeks passed with no word from the runaways. Three times the moon grew large, three times it shone down in shimmering brightness on the swift Curaray, but still there were no signs of Dayuma. Often Akawo would walk far into the forest, looking for footprints along the trails and on the beaches. She knew Dayuma's well, but she saw nothing resembling the familiar track. At night she would steal away from the fire and the hammocks and go as far as she could without danger of being attacked by a jaguar, and listen. Perhaps Dayuma would come quietly through the trees after dark. But days and nights came and went, and her daughter did not return.

Had she been killed by a wild animal? Or had she starved to death out in the forest? Had she reached the world of the foreigners? Had they killed her—and perhaps eaten her? Tyaento had loved his daughter, and Akawo knew of his advice that Dayuma flee when Moipa speared him. Now she alone lived to be concerned for her daughter.

After three long months of watching, Akawo could no longer bear the strain. She must know about her daughter. She commissioned Omiñia, Dayuma's step-grandmother, and young Wiñaemi and her mother to search for Dayuma.

"Look well for her," Akawo said. "Go far downriver and along the beaches. If an animal has eaten her flesh, look for her skeleton along the trails. If you don't find her in our land, go to the outside to the foreigners and look for her. Go until you find some sign of her, and bring me word again."

The little party of three set off through the trees and down the river, following the trail which Dayuma, Umi, and Aepi had taken three months before. Their keen eyes scanned the beaches for familiar footprints. They looked and listened, poling far downriver. One day they heard noises in the forest—the hacking and cracking of trees being cut. There was the shot of a gun. Frightened as a deer, Wiñaemi's mother jumped quickly from the canoe, swam through the water, and disappeared into the forest on the other side. But old Omiñia and Wiñaemi poled the canoe to the side of the river and waited. Perhaps the foreigners were not shooting at them.

Then the foreigners spotted them and came over and talked. But Ominia and Wiñaemi could not understand these strangers. They chattered like monkeys! The men were kind and offered them food. Tired and hungry, Ominia and Wiñaemi accepted their hospitality. Afterward, the foreigners gave them a place for the night. Later the men took Ominia and Wiñaemi downriver, then up another river. After several months they came to an open place, beyond the forest, where there were many more foreigners—and there was Dayuma, living well in a big house! She persuaded them to stay at the hacienda.

Meanwhile, Wiñaemi's mother had returned alone to Akawo with no word from Dayuma. Neither could she tell what had happened to Ominia and Wiñaemi after she herself fled in fright into the forest.

༄ ༄ ༄ ༄

Akawo, struggling to feed her brood of fatherless children, had no way of knowing of the difficulties that followed Dayuma even beyond reach of the sharp spears. The pangs of homesickness that had driven Dayuma to attempt a return to her widowed mother in the first months at the hacienda were deadened by exhausting labor that brought welcome sleep each night.

After several years had elapsed, another way of escape attracted Dayuma. A young Quichua worker at the hacienda, Miguel, asked her to marry him and live down on the Curaray. This broke the pattern of daily drudgery from which there seemed no release. For a time, Dayuma was very happy.

But six months after Dayuma's second son was born, tragedy suddenly struck again. The family was infected with measles—a disease for which jungle Indians have little resistance. Miguel, burning with fever, soon died, followed by the baby boy, and Dayuma wavered between life and death for many days. During her illness, she lost all her hair when the high temperature threatened to claim her life.

Dayuma's dead baby lay on the mat beside her with no one to bury him. The Quichua settlement was also struggling to survive the epidemic. Finally, a neighbor came and buried the baby beside his father. Stunned by grief, Dayuma lost all desire to live. She was too depressed to care, even for her older son, and longed only to be buried with her husband and baby. In her despair, she attempted to take her own life.

*If I could get down to the river, I would drown myself,* she thought. But she was too weak even to crawl to the water.

*Then I will starve myself,* she decided. For two days she ate nothing, but life still refused to loosen its hold.

*Why can't I die?* she wondered in anger.

When Dayuma realized that she wasn't going to die, she began to think of living again. Jacinta, a Quichua woman in the next village and a relative of Miguel's, had offered to care for her if she could get to her home. Dayuma crawled slowly over the long trail to the woman's house. There she was faithfully cared for by Jacinta and her little daughter Maruja, who looked after Dayuma when her mother went to the fields. The child brought her gourds of yuca or banana drink as she lay on her bamboo bed.

It was many months before she was strong enough to return to work at Hacienda Ila. Across from the hacienda lived Olimpia, Miguel's aunt, who offered Dayuma and her son a home.

Just as Dayuma began to regain a foothold in her life, death struck again. Olimpia was suddenly snatched from Dayuma. This was a staggering blow—almost too heavy even for Dayuma's strong spirit. Despondent and still under the influence of liquor customarily consumed at Indian funerals, Dayuma went to Señor Sevilla and asked for a gun to kill Moipa. She had for the moment almost forgotten that Señor Sevilla had selected her to teach the foreigner her language. The first days of instruction had been interrupted by Olimpia's death and funeral.

As Auca study was resumed, Dayuma's sadness began to pass. She found an unexpected motive for living in her friendship with the señoritas. This friendship had opened a peephole into a new kind of fascinating life. Through conversation first with Catherine in Quichua and later in Auca with Rachel, Dayuma began to learn things that she had never heard in the forest, nor at Hacienda Ila. She began to anticipate eagerly the few hours she was free to teach her language to this strange foreigner who wanted to learn Auca but didn't speak Quichua. It became a game, and Dayuma joined the fun with zeal.

Then came the days when Dayuma had remembered enough of her childhood language to teach Rachel to speak Auca. Communication was on a simple level, to be sure, but coherent enough to give Dayuma important clues to unanswered questions. Maybe at last she had found someone who could tell her things which she had wanted to know for years. Her curiosity about God and His carving grew through Rachel's efforts to tell her what the carving meant. Dayuma struggled to remember more Auca so that Rachel could tell her more about God.

Suddenly, in June 1955, when they seemed to be gaining momentum in Auca conversation, Rachel had to leave. This turn of events was hard for Rachel to understand, much less explain to Dayuma. But Rachel and Catherine knew that current circumstances were clearly the Lord's signal for departure.

"Will you come back?" Dayuma asked wistfully as Rachel turned to go.

With faith in the God who had sent her to Dayuma, Rachel replied, "*Otyae imaenti pongimo*—Returning I will come back."

# CHAPTER EIGHT

# Post-Palm Beach

Months of serious illness and other delays hindered Rachel's return to the hacienda. Finally, in March 1956, she and her new partner, Mary Sargent, found themselves on a jungle trail trudging toward Ila. River conditions had made the landing of the float plane impossible, and the overland route was the only way in. Catherine Peeke had gone to the States for furlough, but Mary was happy to replace her as Rachel's partner.

The long, hot trail to Ila provided many hours for reflection and anticipation. Much had happened since Rachel had left the hacienda the year before. In the multitude of thoughts that crowded into her mind, two questions kept cropping up.

Would Dayuma actually be at the hacienda? Although Señor Sevilla had cordially invited Rachel to return, she had heard that Dayuma was away from the hacienda.

How would she talk to Dayuma about Palm Beach? How much would the Auca girl know about the massacre of the five missionaries, including Rachel's brother Nate, three months before? From all that Rachel had learned about the Auca pattern of killing foreigners, there was no doubt in her mind that Dayuma's people had killed her brother. If Dayuma knew this, would it cause strained feelings? Would Dayuma expect Rachel to avenge the death of her brother?

The death of the five men at Palm Beach, the code name for the spot on the Curaray River where they were killed on January 8, 1956, had been a shock to Rachel, as it was to the whole world.* Now on the trail back to Ila, the memory of the little yellow plane that used to fly over and drop mail from home brought alternate waves of pain and joy as Rachel thought of Nate. From the moment that she heard of the death of her brother, she wondered about a connection with Dayuma's family. Would Nate's pictures of Palm Beach provide clues for eventually finding those relatives from whom there had been no sign or sound for nearly nine years?

Immediately after Palm Beach, Rachel wrote to her parents:

"Among the things brought back by the ground expedition is a picture found in Nate's camera of the two Auca women who first came with one Auca man. I keep wondering if they could be Dayuma's mother and younger sister....

"For you two, so far away, we pray the Holy Spirit's comforting. I told the Lord I was willing to make *any sacrifice* to reach these Indians—and this is the first thing He has asked of me. As you know, Nate was precious to me. We rejoice that he is in the Lord's presence now....

"May God yet give me the privilege of going to these same Indians and translating His precious Word for them and seeing the harvest from the five grains of wheat planted way down on the Curaray River in Auca soil."

By the time Rachel could return to the Oriente, many pictures taken by the five men had been published. Which of these had Dayuma seen, and what had been her reaction? Rachel had pictures of the Auca gifts retrieved from the bucket Nate had dropped from the plane. Regarding the pictures, Rachel had written, "I felt so near the Aucas handling the gifts they put in the little basket attached to the bucket—ear plugs, seed ornaments, a beautiful feather headdress,

---

* The story of the martyrdom of Nate Saint, Jim Elliot, Pete Fleming, Roger Youderian, and Ed McCully is told in detail in *Through Gates of Splendor* by Elisabeth Elliot (Tyndale, 1956, 1957, 1981). See also *Shadow of the Almighty* by Elisabeth Elliot (Harper, 1958).

peanuts, cotton, a parrot—all things for which I have words in the language!"

Should she discuss those Auca articles with Dayuma if she was at the hacienda?

As Rachel and Mary rounded the last bend of the trail and came in view of the hacienda, Rachel's first big question was suddenly answered. Dayuma had spotted Rachel and came running out to meet her, giggling with delight and chattering away in Auca.

"You came back!" she exclaimed. "You didn't die!"

Then she told Rachel that she had been wishing and watching for her return for many moons.

"Sometimes I would go out by myself and call to the air, 'Rachel! Come back!'"

In those first few hours of joyous reunion, all of Rachel's wonderings were swept away.

It was easy to talk about Palm Beach, since the widespread publicity had thoroughly penetrated back into the Oriente, where the story began. Dayuma had seen the pictures and knew that they were her very own people. As a matter of fact, she had immediately recognized the older woman who had come to Palm Beach as Aunt Mintaka, her mother's sister. She thought that the man known as "George" was a relative who had grown up in her home. She wanted to believe that the young girl "Delilah" was her younger sister Gimari, but try as she would, she could not. No, it couldn't be Gimari. Gimari was a very little girl when Dayuma left the forest—she couldn't have changed that much! And if Aunt Mintaka lived, perhaps her mother, Akawo, and Gimari lived too, somewhere in the forest!

The pictures and the conversation about them transported Dayuma back to the land of her childhood. This was the first glimpse of home in nine years—almost tangible hope that some of her family still lived.

Rachel wrote her parents,

"I wish you could have seen Dayuma's face when she saw the color picture I took of all the things Nate brought back in the basket. She named them all—each type of basket-weaving, etc. I kept wondering about the tiny houses around the big house in Nate's photos. Now I know—a monkey house, a parrot house, a *guacamayo* house! Dayuma's face brightened at the recollection."

Within a few days of their arrival at Ila, Rachel and Mary moved with the Sevilla family and Dayuma to Hacienda San Carlos, their new location on the Anzu River. With the move, Rachel observed a significant change in Dayuma's position. She had graduated from the status of "hewer of wood and drawer of water" to the rank of house girl. Her duties in the main house of the hacienda enabled Rachel to see her more frequently than when she had spent long hours in the yuca fields or gathering firewood. But language-study hours were irregular because of her obligations.

Of her new acquaintance, Mary Sargent wrote, "We call Dayuma 'the Patchwork Girl' from the Wizard of Oz because she wears a dress now, and it has several patches both front and back. When Rachel and Cathy were here before, she worked in the fields and wore the traditional Indian blouse and skirt. Then one day the family took her to the city and she came back wearing a dress. She waits on the table now as only a 'Patchwork Girl' can, running back and forth in her bare feet like a padded doll! Her ears are pierced, and the holes in the lobes enlarged by the type of ear adornment she used to wear, but her straight black hair cut off at the shoulders hides that mark of identification. Her eyes are smiling and friendly—they can be serious, too. She's an extrovert, impish, alert, a good teacher, and we love her."

Rachel wrote to her parents of the renewed opportunity to work with Dayuma and of her hopes for the Auca tribe:

"The picture has changed considerably. A year ago we were the only ones taking an active step toward learning the Auca language, and now the whole world is interested. This has made it exceedingly difficult for me. I will appreciate your special prayer that the Lord will enable me to do my part quietly. I have no desire for publicity—but I do feel I should continue with Dayuma. I have a love for her and she for me, and the Lord knows my heart. Nate himself always hoped the way would be made for me to reach the tribe....."

But the days of "quietly" doing her part were gone forever as the eyes of the world focused upon the forest-hidden tribe of killers.

The pressures resulting from Palm Beach publicity complicated the program of Auca study which Rachel had hoped to follow. Many travelers found their way to the eastern jungle of Ecuador. A steady trickle of curiosity seekers, adventurers, and some desiring commercial gain from firsthand information began to seep into the hacienda. Great pressures were exerted on Señor Sevilla to share Dayuma's scant free time. Her value as an Auca speaker was evident.

"All the forces of good and evil have converged upon the Aucas," wrote Rachel to close friends who were praying about the situation. "God has shown us in a very personal way the value He has put on this tribe. Now more than ever we need those who will stand with us and pray."

She wrote to another friend, "I told Mary I'd like to write a book of things just as they are happening day by day. She said, 'No one would believe you!' Every once in a while I say, 'The plot sickens'—but we expect a wonderful climax someday!"

The golden opportunity for language study that seemed to be theirs upon arrival soon began to fade into almost no study time with Dayuma. There were days when she did not appear and was seen only as she trotted in and out of the breezeway, serving the table. She was near, but unavailable for teaching her language. Rachel's diary entry for April 2 suggests the struggle:

"Easter Day has come and gone. I meditated on the resurrection—verses that say a spirit has not flesh and blood. Contemplated my kid brother in Gloryland; prayed for the folks at home, and Marj and the children especially. Looked away across the ridge and then at the four Auca women and Dayuma's half-Auca boy who all seem so precious to me. Prayed for faith to continue without discouragement. Only the Lord can prosper the work while we're hearing the language only about three hours a week—but He can, or He can change the circumstances…. Perhaps before next Easter we will be able to tell Dayuma."

There were frequent references in the diary to the ridge and the desire to go "beyond the ridge, where our hearts are." But Rachel knew that she could not go until she could speak Auca.

Furthermore, there was the imminent threat of losing Dayuma completely, for her services as a guide into Auca territory were being sought. However, Dayuma's own hesitation at reentering her tribe where brutal customs had not changed gave her pause. Rachel was surprised at the answer the girl gave Señor Sevilla one day when he proposed an Auca trip: "When God tells me to go, I will go."

Meanwhile, there were others interested in reaching the tribe with the Gospel who felt that more contacts should be attempted. Some felt that Dayuma could fly over and by use of a loudspeaker invite her people to come out. The idea appealed to Dayuma, for she was very eager to go up in a plane. In a letter answering a request for Dayuma's cooperation, Rachel presented reasons for delaying such a project:

"In spite of all the pressures that would seem to indicate that this is the time to make another attempt, from our standpoint here, it seems to me to be premature. There are several circumstances that would point to that. First, Dayuma is still unsaved, and no one could be quite sure just what she would say if she got that near to the people who have killed so many of her family. When we were here before, she expressed a deep hatred for them.

"If she did give a message now, our language work has not progressed sufficiently to be sure exactly what she did say. There are still many words in the language to which we cannot yet assign a definite meaning. We wish we had more time with Dayuma so that the work would progress faster, but so far the Lord has not opened up the way.

"Another big question in my mind is whether it would be right to take the only language teacher available to our cause, and put her in what as your letter expresses might become a dangerous spot. I say that for her sake, since she says plainly that she does not know God, and for our sakes—those of us who are so anxious that her people be reached...."

On a day crowded with many problems, Rachel received heartening news. Dr. Kenneth L. Pike, the linguistic expert under whom she had studied at the Summer Institute of Linguistics in Oklahoma, was in South America to consult with Bible translators about language problems, and offered to visit Rachel and Mary at the hacienda. As an added blessing, Señor Sevilla consented to the extra free time for Dayuma during Dr. Pike's visit. For several days before his arrival, Rachel and Mary worked diligently to assemble all of their Auca data for Dr. Pike to consider.

Rachel recounted the benediction of Dr. Pike's visit in a letter written on May 21 to family and friends:

"Last week Dr. Pike took precious time out of his busy schedule to travel by plane, canoe, and trail to the hacienda. We desperately wanted and needed the help Dr. Pike was able to give us. We talked to Dayuma about his coming. We showed her his picture, recently published in the April 30 issue of *Time* magazine. We told her that he was like our brother....

"When he asked her to repeat and repeat certain words of the language, she patiently did it. In the midst of the phonetic workout, Dayuma asked me, 'Does the Doctor understand my language?' 'No, he understands my language,' I replied. Her only comment was, 'You understand both languages.' "

Pike's skill in repeating and quickly grasping the meanings of Auca words impressed Dayuma and gave Rachel a boost in the analysis of the language. His spiritual counsel and advice lifted the morale of both Mary and Rachel, who had been patiently struggling at times against great odds. Pike encouraged them not to be weary in well-doing but to continue the good fight of faith. Surely, God would reward them in His time.

After Pike's visit, Rachel wrote to her friends:

"There is still so much we don't know how to express in Auca. But I decided that I can talk freely to God about Dayuma, and all the other Aucas fifteen minutes away by air, out in the forest. And someday, because you, too, can talk freely to God about them, may it be that we will be enabled to talk freely to them about Him. Dr. Pike's visit, the added advantage of Mary's help in the tedious analysis of Auca as she works with me here, and the new prayer backing of many Christians now interested in these Indians will surely be used of God to hasten that day.

"After Dr. Pike's visit, I was rechecking my data with Dayuma and came to the word for a bone-instrument which Chief Tariri of the Shapra tribe had given me. Dayuma's Quichua friends, seated on the floor, listened to the discussion in Auca, and asked Dayuma what it was all about. Then she told me in Auca what she had explained to them in Quichua: 'I told them that Tariri made it out of a monkey-bone. That long ago you lived in his house, and learned his language, as you are learning mine, and that now Tariri and his people don't spear anymore. Now they live well with God....' These are the encouraging things for which we praise God...."

Another cause for thanksgiving was the new airstrip at the hacienda that greatly facilitated transportation. Señor Sevilla, who desired the services of the planes of the Instituto Lingüístico de Verano, had ordered it to be built.

As Dayuma thought of the swiftness of travel now possible for Rachel, she asked her one day, "Are you going home to your mother soon?"

"No," Rachel told her, "I would like to visit your mother first, down on the Curaray. But perhaps your people will spear me if I go?"

"If you speak well to them in their language, they won't kill you," Dayuma answered matter-of-factly.

"But I still do not know how to speak their language well. You must teach me every day."

Dayuma said she would.

CHAPTER NINE

# Lazarus

"**W**ho are they?" asked Dayuma one day, holding up a picture of Mary and the baby Jesus.

"This is God's Son, Jesus, and His mother, Mary," answered Rachel.

Rachel told her as best she could about how Jesus came to earth, lived and did good, but was killed, and how He rose from the dead and now lives in heaven with His Father.

"Will He come to earth again?" asked Dayuma, studying the picture again.

"Yes," Rachel replied, "He will come in the clouds, and when He comes again my brother, who is buried on the Curaray, and Don Jaime [Jim Elliott whom Dayuma had met], and the other three who died with them will come to life again and go up to meet Him in the air."

She showed such keen interest that Rachel was encouraged to try more. As Dayuma plied her with questions, Rachel sensed that her interest sprang from her old Auca beliefs concerning death and burial of the body. Other foreigners had gone in at the risk of their lives to find and bury the men who had fallen on the Curaray. This followed a good tribal pattern of burying those who had died by the spear. But what of this new angle to death that she was hearing for the first time? Was it possible that a dead body could come to life again?

Eager to follow up Dayuma's interest in the resurrection of the body, Rachel began to work out a simple explanation in Auca of this basic Scriptural truth. It occurred to her to start with the story of Lazarus. "I worked out the story of Lazarus verse by verse," she later related. "It seemed cumbersome, but late one evening when Dayuma lingered, I felt it was the Lord's time to read it to her. She followed each word, apparently with understanding, but at this stage in language study one can never be quite sure. At Mary's suggestion, I asked Dayuma to tell it back to me. This was her reply: "Lazarus was very sick with fever. Later he died. Martha and Mary cried very much. There was a big stone over the hole, Lazarus being inside. Jesus having come said, "Lazarus, come out fast." He came alive again. Later, cloth untying, he was all well. Very much like God Jesus did."

Mary Sargent, who watched Dayuma's face as she told back the story, recalls, "Her eyes fairly shone! I knew that she was understanding, and I felt that she was believing what Rachel told her. Later I said to Rachel, 'I am sure that Dayuma is born again—she is so responsive!'"

Dayuma's hunger to know more inspired Rachel to translate simple Bible stories into Auca and to begin teaching her the life of Christ. She learned of the miraculous birth and life of Christ, and His power to raise the dead, heal the sick, and still storms. It was all utterly new to Dayuma. Grandfather had never told her stories like these.

Christmas 1956 was crowned with an unexpected joy for Rachel. Dayuma was given permission to accompany her to Quito, where the holidays were spent with Wycliffe and other Christian friends—a novel experience for the jungle girl. The association with people who all believed what Rachel had been telling her left an indelible impression.

Back at the hacienda, Dayuma shared the story of creation and other narratives with Wiñaemi.

"If you teach her about God, she will come to love Him," Dayuma said to Rachel. "Now she loves Him just a little bit. I will tell her lots and then she will come to love Him lots…. Why was I not caused to love Him long ago?"

Such signs of spiritual comprehension encouraged Rachel to believe that Dayuma now had a clear grasp of salvation.

But there was the ever-present barrier to progress in the study of the Auca language: lack of time with Dayuma who was continually busy with necessary hacienda chores. In the early months of 1957, Rachel prayed for more opportunity with her.

One day Rachel was surprised by a radio message from Señor Sevilla, who had gone to Quito. Cameron Townsend was passing through Ecuador and had called upon Sevilla to discuss the Auca work with him. It appeared that Sevilla, known as the "Daniel Boone of Ecuador" because of his amazing experiences with South American Indians, was to participate in a television program featuring the Indians of South America. Dayuma would also appear on the telecast, and Rachel's services as an interpreter would be required. She would have to sharpen up on Auca conversation, so Sevilla was releasing Dayuma for two hours of language work a day.

It seemed a roundabout way of Auca analysis, but Rachel was grateful for any means of learning more. With the unexpected impetus, Rachel's fluency in conversation with Dayuma improved a great deal within a few weeks.

Suddenly, the new schedule was interrupted by a message that left Rachel aghast and reluctant to comply with a request that had been made of her. Would she leave immediately by plane for California with Dayuma to accompany Sevilla on the Daniel Boone television program?

Her first reaction was no—she would not snatch the jungle girl out of her environment and drop her suddenly into Hollywood. The shock would be too much for Dayuma—and what if she should get sick? Rachel objected, anticipating the negative effect of extremely contrasting conditions on Dayuma. It would be like taking her to Mars.

Peace of mind finally came to Rachel when the Lord assured her that the program would provide a means of sharing her own burden for Bible-less tribes with the American public. The fear that Dayuma would die away from her native land was also removed from Rachel's heart.

# CHAPTER TEN

# This Is Your Life

"The big water I saw, I came well," Dayuma was telling Ralph Edwards in her own Auca language. "The stars like light I saw clearly in the big water."

The Auca girl, used to swift-flowing jungle streams, had been impressed by the calm Caribbean over which she had flown en route to California from Ecuador. Airlifted from the backwoods of South America, she now faced the dazzling lights of a Hollywood television studio.

The shock was almost as great for Rachel as it was for Dayuma. In one sense the strain was greater. In a running Auca commentary Rachel was trying to keep Dayuma oriented on the drama of which they were unconsciously the center. The situation was complicated by the fact that Rachel believed that this conversation with Ralph Edwards was only "a rehearsal for a TV interview." Nor did she realize that her life, rather than Sevilla's, was to be featured on Edwards's, "This Is Your Life" program that unforgettable evening of June 5, 1957.

Ralph Edwards had taken Dayuma and Rachel to a platform decorated with palms and a thatched jungle hut. Rachel recollects that he was talking with them casually when—

"Suddenly, from somewhere offstage, I heard my father's voice. I thought that these Hollywood people certainly had gone to a lot of trouble to get him to make a tape recording for me. And then before I knew what was happening, my own dad appeared before me!"

Rachel, suppressing her emotion, took her father over to meet Dayuma. She continues, "Scarcely had I recovered from the shock of my dad's appearance when I heard the voice of my oldest brother, Sam! Then he appeared!"

Sam Saint, an airline captain, had been flown with his father from the East Coast of the United States for the event honoring his missionary sister. As he left the center of the stage, he passed Rachel again, kissed her, and whispered, "Don't make it hard for Ralph, Sis. He's working against time."

"And it was at that point," Rachel says, "that I woke up to the fact that this was the real thing! We were appearing on TV before thousands of viewers!"

Later in the program she heard Ralph Edwards say that thirty *million* people were watching. Almost simultaneous with Rachel's realization of Ralph Edwards's dilemma was his realization that Rachel was having to explain the fast-moving mystery to a bewildered Indian girl who knew no English.

Rachel heard the voice of her lifetime friend Beryl Walsh Adcock, and she too appeared, to Rachel's increased amazement. Then her old friend Dr. Addison Raws of the Keswick Colony of Mercy in New Jersey, with whom Rachel had worked before she went to Peru, emerged from nowhere. Next Lorrie Anderson, her former partner from the Shapra tribe of Peru, walked in. She was followed by Rachel's coworker from Ecuador, Don Burns, who was escorting Señor Sevilla to the lights.

"Señor Sevilla was the only one I wasn't surprised to see," Rachel said after the program, "because I thought the 'interview' was to feature him!"

While yet gasping "at the rapidity with which things happen in Hollywood" she heard yet another voice. "That was the most fantastic of all—when *Tariri* came in to greet me!"

Her good friend the Shapra chief, now a vigorous and radiant Christian, had been flown from the north Peruvian jungle and dropped in the middle of Hollywood to greet his "sister" Rachel.

In a half hour, members of her family and her closest friends from different parts of the world had greeted her—"a group I hadn't ever dreamed of seeing together this side of heaven!"

Masterful poise and presence of mind enabled Ralph Edwards to pilot the program to a successful conclusion, coordinating a motley array of Indians and missionaries who had been living by the sun, not by split-second studio clocks. He had politely but anxiously watched the measured minutes tick away, sensing the problems involved for Rachel and Dayuma, and graciously solving them on the spot.

After the program, Ralph Edwards's guests were escorted to the Hollywood Roosevelt Hotel, where the happy reunion continued with less tension. Understandably, curious patrons of the hotel were fascinated by the befeathered Indian chief and the Auca television star as they were ushered into the lobby. Although the jungle Indians exhibited remarkable poise and aplomb under the exotic circumstances, the fashion and fare of the luxurious hotel were indeed life on another planet for them. When the strain of public pressure began to take its toll, how grateful they were for private rooms with doors. Meals served in their rooms proved to be more successful than dining-room conviviality, complicated for folk of the forest by foreign food and confusing arrays of silverware they did not know how to use. A Wycliffe translator from Los Angeles who had lived in the jungles of Peru sensed the predicament and smuggled a big pot of plain boiled rice and chicken into the hotel for the disoriented Indians. They hungrily devoured it to the last grain.

Dayuma had been delighted to meet Tariri at last, and he was equally happy to meet her. His first question upon seeing her had been, "Does Dayuma know the Lord?" This was his chief concern, far outweighing other features of the exciting evening. He had prayed for her conversion.

Weary but happy, Tariri left Rachel and Dayuma as he turned to go to his elegant room in the hotel.

"Good night, my big sister," he said to Rachel.

Then turning to Dayuma, "Good night, little sister."

The next evening Rachel sat at the bedside of a very sick Indian girl. The shadowy fear which had threatened her in Ecuador lay before her in tangible form. Dayuma was burning with a high fever.

Rachel remembered having met a doctor earlier that evening in the lobby of the hotel. He had been with friends who shared the telecast. Perhaps he was still in the lobby.

Without realizing that Dr. Ralph Byron, Jr., was an eminent cancer specialist, the director of the Tumor Hospital of the City of Hope Medical Center, Rachel was grateful for his prompt arrival in the room where Dayuma lay ill. Neither did Rachel know that Dr. Byron was an earnest Christian who had been praying for Dayuma long before her trip to the United States.

Dr. Byron, with Rachel interpreting, gave Dayuma a simple, direct testimony of his faith in Christ.

"Are you trusting the Lord Jesus, too?" he asked Dayuma in conclusion.

"Yes!" was the spontaneous answer. "I think of Him day and night!"

It was the first testimony of personal faith in the Lord that Rachel had heard from Dayuma's lips. And Rachel caught again the look of radiance which had shone from Dayuma's eyes on first hearing the story of Lazarus.

Dr. Byron prayed quietly, giving thanks to God and requesting healing for the Auca girl.

By morning the fever had disappeared and Dayuma was back to normal.

# CHAPTER ELEVEN

# A Search
# Across Two Continents

$R$achel and Dayuma's stay in the United States was longer than they had planned. The time was exciting but draining, as the Lord opened doors for ministry during their travels, and even provided Rachel with additional extended times of language study with Dayuma.

The duo's travels included a stop in New York, where the Billy Graham evangelistic crusade was in progress. When Graham heard that Rachel and her Auca friend were in the United States, he invited them to give a testimony and report in Madison Square Garden. Questions flooded Rachel's mind. How would she explain to Dayuma that she would be appearing before thousands of people? How would the girl react?

When Rachel suggested that Dayuma tell the huge audience a Bible story in Auca, all reticence left her. She happily selected one of her favorites—the raising of Jairus's daughter. With a great deal of enthusiasm and Auca animation, she recounted the story with gestures, while Rachel translated it into English. The story was joyfully concluded as the young girl was raised to life by Jesus who told her mother to "cook that she might eat. And her parents were very, very, very happy!"

The experience brought much blessing to the New York listeners and to Billy Graham, who was deeply moved by the testimony of the first Auca Christian.

When the invitation to accept Christ was given at the close of the meeting, hundreds found their way to the platform.

Dayuma was amazed that so many people in the United States hadn't already accepted Christ. She had thought all the people in Rachel's land would know the Lord because they had God's carving in their own language. Weeks earlier, after having landed in Miami, Florida, and upon seeing great crowds of Americans, her first question had been, "Do all these people love God?"

Their travels took them next to Philadelphia, where Dayuma finally met Rachel's mother, "who had sent the carving across the big water." As Dayuma met others of the Saint family, she became more convinced that these relatives of the pilot who had been killed by her people had no intention of retaliating, of "killing in exchange." This conviction was later to lead toward opening the door to the Auca tribe. Dayuma had seen the dead foreigner's relatives and talked with them—and they still loved the Aucas.

In a quiet cabin in the pine woods of Pennsylvania, Rachel and her parents spent several happy weeks with Dayuma. The similarity to her own forest home in Ecuador revived many memories, both pleasant and unpleasant. As darkness began to fall each evening, Rachel noticed a return of fear in the girl's eyes. The devil of the forest was lurking near in the big trees, Dayuma warned, and perhaps tonight he would suck their blood! Rachel observed that when swarms of mosquitoes would gather, Dayuma started swatting them frantically. Rachel learned that these insects were considered to be evil spirits, whose bites would bring dire results. The Auca girl, though far from her jungle home, was still haunted by dreadful fears. Hour after hour she would unburden her soul to Rachel, who could now understand and help. But for the casting out of these lifetime fears, Rachel knew that only the power of God Himself was sufficient. Rachel continually prayed for wisdom and guidance, and searched the Scriptures for an antidote to the girl's fears.

The miracles of Jesus in casting out demons in the days of His earthly ministry would prove to be a solution to Auca fears! Rachel told Dayuma the story of the demon-possessed Gadarene whom Jesus pitied and restored to normal life by ordering the demons to leave and enter a herd of swine. The girl listened with great interest, especially to the climax when the swine went tumbling headlong into the sea where they drowned dramatically. That final destruction of the demons, at Jesus' command, indicated that the Savior who lived in her heart was more powerful than witch doctors or demons.

The sequel to the Gadarene story challenged the Auca girl. The Gadarene in his joy and gratitude wanted to stay with Jesus, but was told by the One who had restored him, "Go home to thy friends, and tell them how great things the Lord hath done for thee." He obeyed, and later through his testimony a great crowd came together to hear Jesus when He arrived. Rachel recognized an opportunity to plant the seed of desire for returning to her own home in Dayuma's mind. Perhaps Jesus might someday ask her to go home to her family and friends and tell them of His power. Rachel said she would willingly go to the Aucas—would Dayuma go, too? It was quite evident that the girl was pondering the question. The old fear of Satan's power was beginning to weaken through the constant teaching from God's carving.

In September, Dayuma accompanied Rachel to Wycliffe's biennial meeting in Sulphur Springs, Arkansas, a quiet country village of scarcely five hundred people. This gathering of translators from all over the world was indeed a family reunion for Rachel. Many of her companions in Bible translation, whom she had not seen for years, were in the States on furlough and attending the conference. They were overjoyed to see Rachel, but just as thrilled and moved to see her Auca friend for whom they had prayed. The name *Dayuma* was already familiar to many who had been asking the Lord for her salvation since 1955.

❧ ❧ ❧ ❧

As Rachel stood watch at Dayuma's bedside in Sulphur Springs, she prayed and pondered. The Asian-flu epidemic of 1957 had affected Dayuma, who was unaccustomed to foreign diseases, more gravely than it had most Americans. The girl had grown steadily worse for several days and was burning with fever. Rachel knew she needed help. What should she do?

As she looked to God for guidance, she suddenly remembered that Dr. Kenneth Altig, a Wycliffe doctor from the jungle base in Peru, was on furlough in California. While working with the Shapras, she had often conferred with him by radio across five hundred miles of jungle about sick Indians. He would know better than anyone else what to do for an Auca girl temporarily transplanted to Arkansas. She telephoned him, and in a three-minute conversation he prescribed for Dayuma. Within a few days she passed the crisis and was on the road to recovery.

Dayuma was slow, however, in regaining strength. Rachel kept vigil around the clock, feeding her liquids with a spoon until she was able to sit up and feed herself. One day after Rachel served her a cup of coffee, there was a persistent vibration between the cup and saucer as it rested on the tray.

She saw that the noise was bothering the sick girl, but try as she would, she could not stop it.

"It is the devil of the forest!" Dayuma said apprehensively.

In her weakened condition, the fears of her childhood assailed her with great force.

"The devil is saying in the cup, 'Don't drink me. You'll get worse.'" Dayuma, certain she had been cursed, took the vibration as a warning.

Rachel reminded her of the power of the Lord, who was stronger than the devil. But the noise continued, and Dayuma was not convinced.

"I'm not afraid of the devil because the Lord Jesus lives in me, and I will drink the coffee!" said Rachel finally.

With that, Dayuma rose to the challenge.

"No," she said with resolution, "you talk to the Lord Jesus and *I'll* drink the coffee."

So Rachel prayed, and Dayuma drank the coffee!

More deep-seated fears of Dayuma's childhood were gradually unfolding revealed by her chance remarks and the Auca legends she remembered. One day Dayuma mentioned that devils attacked at night and sucked her people's blood. When Rachel challenged the old Auca belief, the girl objected, "But you said that Satan was 'chief of the devils.'"

Rachel found that Dayuma was combining the biblical doctrine concerning Satan with what she had learned in her childhood. Again, through patient teaching, Dayuma began to see that Satan's desire was to destroy the souls of men. The climactic assurance from God's carving that "greater is he that is in you, than he that is in the world" inspired Dayuma with new confidence in her battle with the old fears.

During her slow recuperation, the teaching of the Word translated orally into Auca began to penetrate her thinking deeply.

Gradually, Dayuma's faith in God grew, and the fears subsided. One night she dreamed she was back at Hacienda Ila, and her old companions were tempting her to sin. In her dream she answered them, "No, now I belong to the Lord—I don't live like that anymore." In another dream the powers of evil were pressing down and threatened to overcome her. She told Rachel that in the name of the Lord Jesus she ordered the devils to leave—and they did. She was applying the teaching of the book of Acts. This spiritual gain compensated for the precious time Rachel had expected to invest in concentrated linguistic study.

In those critical days, the assurance given Rachel before leaving Ecuador that the Auca girl would not die in the States was a comfort when she would have despaired of Dayuma's life. As in Hollywood when Dayuma had been very ill, the Lord revived her body.

It was not until early November that Dayuma was able to walk again and enjoy fairly normal activity. Her progress, though slow, was steady. With no unforeseen complications, Rachel knew that soon she would be able to resume study of Auca grammar. She would wait, however, until the girl was stronger.

On Monday, November 18, very early in the morning, the tranquillity of the Ozark "Sleepy Hollow" was abruptly broken by a long-distance telephone call from Rachel's brother Sam in New York. He relayed the breathtaking news from Ecuador that two Auca women had run out of the forest and were on the edge of Auca territory with missionaries. He had few details, but assured Rachel that Marj Saint, who was in California, would be calling her. She doubtless would know more of the story.

Dayuma wondered who the early caller was. When she heard the news, she was puzzled—and pensive. It was a long way from home for such a message. Were these actually her people who had come out of the forest?

Forgetting the time difference between Arkansas and California, and having waited for what seemed a long while to hear from her sister-in-law, Rachel placed a call to Marj Saint. She learned that Betty Elliot, widow of Jim Elliot who had died on Palm Beach, was with the women at the Quichua village on the Curaray where they had emerged from the Auca forest. One was thought to be the older woman who had visited with the five men on Palm Beach. If true, she was Dayuma's Aunt Mintaka. A further detail excited speculation. A third woman, much younger than the other two, had come out with them but had fled back into the forest. Who was she?

"Two women fresh from the tribe who perhaps spoke the same language we were studying!" The thrilling anticipation sent Rachel's hopes soaring and her hands to packing. With the first news flash, she began to prepare for the return trip to Ecuador. As she shared the details of the momentous events with Dayuma, assuming that she, too, would be overjoyed with plans for returning, she sensed the girl's hesitancy. Disappointed, Rachel listened. Even if she did return to Ecuador, Dayuma explained, she was too weak to walk the steep trail to the Curaray. She knew what the trip entailed.

It had not occurred to Rachel that they would not leave immediately, but she saw that the girl was not ready to go.

Dayuma asked many questions, for she had been burdened from the first call. She knew the pattern of her people well. What had prompted them to come out? Was it a decoy?

She appealed to Rachel that the missionaries be urged to take the two women and get out. "My people will surely come and kill," she warned. Her advice was telephoned to Ecuador the same day.

Although Dayuma was hesitant and apprehensive about returning immediately, she experienced an uncontrollable desire for answers to several other questions. Could the woman who had come out with her Aunt Mintaka be her very own mother? And could the younger woman who had fled back into the forest be her younger sister Gimari? The pull was almost irresistible. A possible clue to the whereabouts of her family, after more than a decade of silence! With her people moving from river to river, she had no idea where they might be living now. A delay in returning to Ecuador might mean loss of contact for another ten years.

Rachel knew that hours counted. Her concern was that the women, like the younger girl, might soon flee into the forest. If they did, the questions about Dayuma's mother and her family might never be answered. The missionaries in whose custody they were could not speak their language. It was urgent that Dayuma help.

Rachel suggested that Dayuma make a tape recording to persuade the two women not to run away. Dayuma rose to the occasion. Bundled in a warm robe and seated before the recorder, she trembled with weakness and excitement. In a voice charged with emotion, she delivered a message for her people. She identified herself, pleaded with them not to run away, and asked that they send back an answer giving their names and those of their relatives.

"Long ago when Moipa speared my father," she began, "Umi, Aepi, and I fled to the outside. My father was Tyaento. I am Tyaento's daughter Dayuma. My mother was Akawo....

"Long ago we did not live well, not loving God. The Aucas spoke saying that God created. Our old grandfather said that God created. All men and all women He created. Yes, I now love that God. Now I live very well. Before I did not live well.

"The foreigners who do not love God do not live well. Now those who speak to you, yes, they all speak of God. Very well they speak. You two do not return to the Auca houses. Live in the foreigners' house....

"Now, you, who are you two? I do not know. You two in return speak to me; I will understand. Do not you two be afraid. Live in the foreigners' house. You two will not be afraid. I live without fear. Very well I live.... You are just afraid that the foreigners will shoot and you will die...."

Through the years Dayuma had longed for an end to the constant friction between her people and outsiders. She had hoped for peaceful relations and for a friendly contact to be made. She now urged the two women to encourage such a communication between the two groups.

"Go visiting to the foreigners' houses with your relatives. They will not spear; they will visit well with you. Then the foreigners in return will visit your houses. If the ones that love God visit, they will visit well."

Dayuma knew that she could not endorse the visits of all foreigners, remembering full well that exploiters had ruthlessly killed Aucas. But she urged the women to welcome foreigners like the ones with whom they were living.

"Don't you two return to the forest. A little bit later I will come to your house. There I will speak to you both. Umi and Wiñaemi do not remember our language. It has been a long time since they came, and Wiñaemi was very small when she came to the outside. Now she is grown up. She does not remember the Auca language and understands only the foreigners' speech.

"I remembered a little bit long ago. Then another foreigner came and spoke with me. She, a woman, spoke with me, and I understood. Then in return I spoke with her in my language. Very well I spoke. Now I live with her. Later, returning, I will come.

"Who are you two? I in exchange will understand. You two speak with me. When the ones you live with say, 'Speak,' do not be afraid to speak."

In a detailed account of her family, relatives, and others of her group, Dayuma told what she knew of each of them. She named those who had gone to the outside and died, and those who she believed were still living. The names of her relatives would unmistakably identify Dayuma to the two Auca women.

"My uncle is Wamoñi, my other uncle is Gikita. My mother's little sister is Gami, Umi's mother. My mother's sisters born later were Wiika, Wiwa, and Mintaka.

"What rivers do you live on? Do you live now on Fish River or on Palm River? I have not returned for a long time to your huts. Does my mother live? I don't know. It has been so long that I don't remember all the other Aucas. Tell me who still lives, and I will understand. I was not able to return. I lived in another foreigner's house. I told him I would return to my people. He was angry. Now in another house I live well. That is all."

During the anxious days after the tape was sent, news coming from the Curaray was not good. There were constant signs of Aucas lurking nearby, which the Quichua Indians and the missionaries interpreted as threats.

Dayuma reacted fearfully to every report. Well she knew the spot on the Curaray where the Auca women had taken refuge first with Quichua Indians and later with missionaries. It had been the home of Dayuma's husband, Miguel. Not far away he and her baby son were buried. It was there that Dayuma in deep sorrow had tried to take her own life.

The news recalled other events from the past: of death, of unhappy encounters with foreigners on the edge of Auca territory, of thwarted efforts to locate the trail that would lead to her home in the forest.

Then came the word that Dayuma had dreaded. Her people had appeared and killed the Quichua Indian who had first received the two Auca women. His body had been riddled with twenty-two spears. His young wife had been taken captive.

After hearing the tragic report, Dayuma began to relax. "Now my people will not come again. They will hide in the forest."

Further word was received that Betty Elliot had taken the two women and gone to Shandia, a safe distance from the scene of the spearing. In a letter to Catherine Peeke, who was in Ecuador, Rachel wrote, "Dayuma is sleeping now—in the sleep of sorrow, I guess. Dear girl! She dreamed of spearings and attacks every night and never really relaxed until she heard that the women were in Shandia."

Tension that had been high for two weeks was finally released. With the release, however, came an added concern. From the heart of the jungle far across the big water had come the news of how her people had speared, almost as soon as it happened. How could news about her people travel so far so *fast?* Rachel explained that Christian friends, people who were praying and who were interested in the Aucas, had sent the word by radio.

But further details of the killing worried the girl. She had been suffering with those involved, but at a helpless distance. The young wife who had been captured was Maruja, the daughter of Jacinta, the Quichua woman who had nursed Dayuma back to health after her husband and son had died. Maruja was the little girl who had brought her gourdfuls of banana or yuca drink when her mother went to the fields. Now that girl, a young widow, was a captive of Dayuma's people.

"The man who lost a woman took a woman," was Dayuma's natural explanation. She was certain that the husband of one of the women had taken Maruja.

Dr. Wilfred Tidmarsh, the missionary living closest to Auca territory, had recorded the speech of the Auca women when they first arrived at the Curaray settlement. Word had been sent that a copy of the tape was on its way to Sulphur Springs, but to Rachel and Dayuma it seemed that the package from Ecuador would never come. Finally the tape arrived. Dayuma could hardly wait for Rachel to set up the recorder.

To Rachel's dismay, her copy of the Auca conversations was made over a vigorous piano concerto previously recorded and not erased. Each time there was something particularly vital to hear, very loud bass parts of the concerto boomed forth.

Over the obscuring strains of the piano solo and through pitiful sobs and sighs, the Auca voices poured out a lamentation of spearings and killings, of sufferings and fears. Using the phrases and words of Auca previously recorded by Dayuma, Dr. Tidmarsh had questioned the women, and their answers were a tangle of classical chords and rapid, nasalized Auca, charged with high emotion.

Rachel had wondered if the language of the two women would be in the same dialect studied with Dayuma. The first phrases of the tape were muddled, then suddenly through an acoustic clearing she understood the phrase, "Being an orphan I came..."

Rachel rejoiced! Meanwhile, Dayuma was glued to the recorder and would permit no interruptions for clarification or questions. Rachel longed to stop the machine to listen again to an obscure phrase, but Dayuma was too eager for word from home.

"Who is speaking?" Dayuma kept asking as she listened intently. "Is it my mother?" The possibility, overshadowed with uncertainty, seemed almost more than she could bear.

Interspersed among the strains of the concerto and the sobs were vital bits of information that Dayuma began to piece together. Although the near-hysterical speaker did not give her name, she told enough family history for Dayuma to identify her as Maengamo, Uncle Gikita's wife. And Uncle Gikita was Dayuma's mother's brother! Maengamo also divulged that her younger brother had come with her out of the forest, but for fear of the foreigners, had fled immediately. Which of Maengamo's brothers was it—Kimo or Dabu? They were both like brothers to Dayuma, since they had been brought up in her home. And Maengamo's companion was Mintaka—why, that was Dayuma's mother's *sister!*

When Dr. Tidmarsh mentioned Dayuma's name to the two women, there was no answer except the piano concerto, and then Maengamo broke out in the nasalized, rhythmic song that the four Auca girls had sung at Ila. This was a severe disappointment, since Rachel and Dayuma had hoped for a favorable response at the mention of the name "Dayuma."

Maengamo's monologue was concerned with past spearings in the tribe, details of Tyaento's spearing, the horrible atrocities of Moipa, and an impassioned tirade against the hated killer. Moipa had been speared, but Maengamo did not say that he had been speared *dead*. Was the murderer of her father still alive, after all the intervening years since Dayuma had left the forest?

To Rachel's dismay, the Auca girl who had been progressing in victory over the old hates and fears was being sucked back into the old tribal maelstrom of anger and revenge.

Maengamo referred repeatedly to her fear of foreigners, and said that she and her companion were "throwing themselves" on Dr. Tidmarsh's mercy.

Aunt Maengamo told of how an airplane—"a foreigners' wood-bee"—had circled their huts and of how the Aucas called out to it, as if it could understand what they were saying. She mentioned that her people had heard a chopping sound in the forest and had said, "Let's go see." She spoke of a vine dropped down from the wood-bee.

The incoherent tragedy sobbed out on the tape threw Dayuma into a state of nervous high tension. As she listened again and again to the garbled message, the girl's spirits plunged to the depths of sadness. She began to relive the grim horrors of her childhood. By day and by night she was under the shadow of the old spears. At times when the emotional tempest threatened to swallow Dayuma, Rachel would suggest a long, quiet walk in the Ozark woods, where Shetland ponies and fattened pigs served as soothing tranquilizers. After a relaxing break, they would tackle the tape again.

The transcription of the tape was a major accomplishment. The Auca speech was much faster than Dayuma's, and was much more nasalized. There were new Auca words and phrases. Rachel analyzed and translated the tape phrase by phrase, asking Dayuma to repeat some of the rapid phrases in slower Auca. The girl also explained the new vocabulary in words familiar to Rachel. It was an exhausting assignment for one who had never heard Auca spoken in a natural context, as well as for Dayuma, who had not heard her mother tongue for many, many years.

In those days, Rachel discovered other chambers in the great hall of horrors of the tribe to which she was called. She prayed earnestly for spiritual and mental equilibrium for Dayuma as the turbulence of her past dashed upon her mercilessly. At times the Indian girl was distracted by the haunting questions, "Does my mother live? Does my sister live?"

Rachel dreaded the news that the next tape from Ecuador might bring—if indeed the two women had not run back into the forest.

By praying with Dayuma and teaching her line upon line God's will as revealed in the Bible, she endeavored to fortify the storm-tossed soul against any stronger onslaught.

On Thanksgiving Day, Rachel was cheered by a spontaneous prayer revealing Dayuma's desire for her own people, in spite of mental torment: "Let those who know about You speak to others. Then they will understand. If the Aucas aren't angry, we will return and tell them about God. You gave us that we might eat. Your Son in exchange died."

# CHAPTER TWELVE

# A Bruised Reed

In those days of stress and suspense, Rachel was frequently reminded that faithful friends were praying for Dayuma and her tribe. One who had remembered them for many years was Dr. Raymond Edman, president of Wheaton College and former missionary to the Oriente of Ecuador. As a personal friend of the Saint family, he had known the circumstances that led Rachel to the Auca tribe, and had followed her work with keen interest and constant prayer. He and a fellow missionary, Reuben Larson (later cofounder of the Pioneer Missionary Broadcasting Station HCJB), had pioneered in the jungles of Ecuador. Through the years they had not ceased to beseech God for an opening of the Auca tribe to the Gospel.

On December 24, 1957, Dr. Edman wrote Rachel:

"Often we have been looking upward for Dayuma and you. Last evening Reuben and Grace Larson were with us for dinner, and a large part of our conversation was about the latest developments on the Oglán. Interesting indeed that the two Aucas who have come are related to Dayuma. The light begins to penetrate the darkness!"

The Larsons had gone to the Oriente in 1924 in the hope of reaching the Aucas with the Gospel. They had heard of the merciless killers, "without God and without hope."

"Our part has been taking one step toward them into the jungle," Grace Larson later wrote to Rachel. "To you has been given the priceless privilege of accomplishment, the blood, the sweat, and the tears."

The Larsons had kept three of thirty-nine chonta spears that had been used to pin a Quichua Indian to the ground near their mission station in the jungle. These spears were to them "vivid reminders of men without God."

Although ill health forced the Larsons to leave the jungle, they had never ceased to pray for the tribe whose needy condition drew them to Ecuador. And through the years their prayer fellowship with the Edmans for the Aucas had continued. Now years later, in 1957, they were rejoicing in the slight shaft of light penetrating the deep Auca darkness.

After Christmas a second taped installment of the tragedy arrived in Sulphur Springs from Ecuador. It was a continuation of the fears and sorrows of the first—without the piano concerto. Maengamo, always the main speaker, said she had left the fears of the tribe behind, mindful of other fears before her in the outside world. Her second daughter had been killed by witchcraft—a fate certain to be hers also if she remained in the forest. She was quite sure that the foreigners would shoot with their "made things," or that they would eat her alive—but she had come anyway. "They will cut you up alive and eat you cooked" had been the warning when she decided to leave.

"I buried my daughter and came," she wailed over the tape.

With hysterical blubberings, she jumped from the present to the past in her endless recounting of killings and curses.

Then came the word for which Dayuma had long waited. Moipa had been speared dead years ago! With agonizing detail, Maengamo depicted the treachery which had ended in Moipa's awful death. "They were as mad as *iwa* monkeys when they speared Moipa," she said.

Dayuma gave a shout of joy, and it hurt Rachel that she was so happy over any spear-killing. Jubilation turned to sorrow a few minutes later as she heard tragic word about her family. Her big brother Wawae, who was her favorite, had been murdered a long time ago. Dayuma had begun talking about returning to the Auca forest, and was counting on living with him. "He always brought me meat from the forest. I loved him very much," she said.

Dayuma's tears began to fall as Maengamo gave all the cruel details of her big brother's death. As she wept, she listened for more news of her family. But there was not a word about her mother, nor her sisters. Again, the tape poured out more accounts of Moipa's heartless spearings.

The sobs of sorrow gave way to tears of anger as Dayuma thought of those who had killed Wawae. Old fires of hatred and resentment leaped into flame.

"I will never go back!" wailed Dayuma. Her last hope had been dashed. There was no one to go to, not even Wawae. Surely, her mother had been speared, and there was no word of her sisters.

In a firm voice, Rachel began to check the rising anger which threatened to undo the spiritual progress of recent weeks. Spasms of violent weeping exhausted the heartsick girl as Rachel reasoned with her. She reminded her that the Lord Jesus had left heaven to come to earth where people hated Him and finally murdered Him. But what did He do when He was being killed? He loved his enemies and forgave them!

Love your enemies...forgive them.... Those concepts were not in Auca thinking. It was a hard lesson for Dayuma to learn in the heat of the battle.

Rachel continued, "If the Lord Jesus had not left heaven, we would never have heard of Him. You are the *only* one of your people who knows God. How will they hear if you don't go to tell them? You may be the *only* one who can tell them of Jesus." Dayuma was thinking it over, but she was still angry, very angry, with Moipa and the others who had killed Wawae.

Rachel also reminded her that the Bible taught, "Let not the sun go down upon your wrath"—and the sun was about to go down in Sulphur Springs. That was a difficult command at the end of a very sad day. But as the darkness began to settle upon the little village, Dayuma reached a momentous decision.

"Not being angry I will sleep," she said quietly.

In that time of spiritual crisis, when the passion for revenge was being replaced in Dayuma by a desire to forgive, she listened carefully to the Bible lessons chosen for the occasion, and made personal applications. Rachel told her the complete story of David, including Saul's designs upon his life. David did not retaliate, but trusted God to deal with his enemy in *His* way.

"Dayuma became so interested in the story that she kept wanting to know more," Rachel recalls. "She pushed me beyond what I felt I was capable of teaching. When I would come to a stopping place, she would say, 'And then?'"

So it was that she heard the whole long, sad story of the kings of Israel, reinforced by Rachel with related admonitions from other parts of the Bible. "Rejoice not when thine enemy falleth" was a timely word. "Vengeance is mine, I will repay, saith the Lord," underscored the lesson. David's life gave Dayuma food for thought for many days.

On the tape from Ecuador, Dayuma had heard the name of one of Moipa's relatives who escaped the spearings that wiped out his family.

"I could find him when I return and tell him about God," Dayuma said thoughtfully one day.

It was Rachel's turn to shout for joy! This, indeed, was genuine victory—a token of God-taught forgiveness. Love was beginning to replace the old Auca pattern of hate.

Later, after a discussion concerning the kings of Israel and their shortcomings, Dayuma prayed, "God, You alone become the Aucas' Chief."

In January 1958, the English translation of the second involved message from Maengamo and Mintaka was finished and sent back to those in Ecuador who were eagerly awaiting the next chapter.

As Rachel dropped the package in the mail, she noticed the date: January 8. She thought back two years. On January 8, 1956, her brother Nate and four of his friends had laid down their lives for Dayuma's people. And already the first message about God in Auca had been sent back to two other members of the tribe. In those two years, Rachel had learned to communicate with Dayuma in Auca, and had led her gently to a love and knowledge of the living God.

There was good evidence that as a child of God she was maturing in her Christian life. The travail and the trials had not been in vain.

Rachel remembered the watch night service in the Wycliffe home in Quito on the eve of 1957. As various members of the group voiced their petitions to God, Mary Sargent had asked Him for something which startled Rachel. She confidently requested that during 1957 there might be a fruitful contact with the tribe. Now Rachel recalled Mary's prayer of faith which God had honored. It was in November of that year that Dayuma's aunts had run out of the forest. Rachel remembered another prayer—one she uttered on January 1, 1956. She had asked the Lord to reach the Auca tribe "with me or without me," adding that she was willing to make any sacrifice to that end. A week later her beloved brother Nate died on Auca soil. She traced God's hand in the events of the last two years. His ways had proved to be higher than hers, and His sovereign purposes were being realized.

A convincing proof of divine planning was the continued presence of Dayuma's relatives with Betty Elliot. Although separated by thousands of miles from Dayuma and Rachel, communication by tape and written message kept the aunts waiting hopefully for Dayuma's appearance. One day a letter from Betty arrived with a picture of Mintaka and Maengamo enclosed. The strong homeward pull from the pictures brought tears to Dayuma's eyes—tears of joy at the sight of her very own kin.

"Let me talk to them!" she said eagerly. "I want to speak to my relatives!" Rachel quickly obliged and set up the tape recorder. From a heart overflowing with a new love for her own people, Dayuma sent a personal message unconsciously reflecting her desires for them. After encouraging them to stay with Betty Elliot where they would "live well," she promised to come to them later.

"Maengamo, Mintaka, you two live there in another foreigner's house. In the same way, I live here with lots of other foreigners. You two stay with the tall foreign woman. Follow her, do not go to another house. Stay with the tall white woman. She has one child and is a widow. If you two go to another house, it will not be good. I speak, and you two listen to me. My name is Dayuma.

"I lived in the house where you are now for three days. Now I live in the house of another who is like her relative. Here, far away, on the other side of the big water I live. Later, returning, I will come.

"Maengamo, why didn't you speak straight? I could not understand. You only said that long ago they killed. You spoke about my grandfather who was killed. Tell me about the ones who live! Tell me where they live. 'Here they live, here he lives'—tell me. Don't just tell me about those who were speared long ago. Does my mother live? I don't know. Did they spear her? I don't know.

"Now Umi, Wiñaemi, and Omiñia live not far from where you two live now. Close by they live. Why don't you visit with them? I can't come now. I will come later.

"There where you live now they all sing, there in their singing-house. You two go there and hear about God who lives high in the sky. The Aucas say that long ago God created men and women. They didn't remember more. Where does God live? 'We don't know,' they said. Who created the water? 'God created the water. God created everything,' they said. They didn't remember any more.

"The Aucas don't live well. God lives high in the sky. Long ago His Son was born as a child. We did not live well, we sinned. We slept with other men. We shouldn't do it. It is not good. Don't you two live like that. It is true that I lived that way before; I did not live well. I didn't know about God; I didn't understand. Now I understand, and now I am happy. There was no one to tell me. I just lived. Now I understand; now I live well.

"When we did not live well, God's Son came to earth. He in exchange died. After three days He came to life. Now He lives high in the sky. Very well He lives.

"When, returning, will He come? Maybe at night, in the daytime, at noontime—we don't know. Inside the earth lots and lots of fire blazes. Yes, it's awful. When He comes, those who sin will live there. If we love God when we die, we will go high in the sky where He is thatching a beautiful hut for us. Here in our hut we will die. Yes, our flesh will rot. Our souls will go high in the sky. It is very beautiful there!

"God's Son was born on the earth. His mother was an unmarried woman. His Father, God, lives high in the sky. Later, after God's

Son was born, He became mature. He came to one who was blind. He touched his eye with His hand, and that one saw. Another had a lame foot and could not walk. God's Son touched him and he became better fast—then he walked rapidly! Another died, and God's Son said, 'Get up—stand up!' And he stood up! God's Son did very well. He loves everybody. He loves all of the Aucas. He loves them very much.

"Even though He did well, some people said that He was a witch doctor. Some did not speak well of Him. He is not a witch doctor; He is God's Son. Do not be afraid of the devils. God's Son speaks to the devils. 'Go!' He says. And they flee! They are afraid of Him. The devils lived inside of a man's flesh. Seeing Him, they were afraid. 'You are God's Son,' they said. 'Don't come here.' Then they said, 'We are many. In whose flesh will we live? We will enter the flesh of wild hogs!' Then they entered the wild hogs. They ran into a lake and were all drowned. The wild hogs died with the devils. God does very well. Don't you two be afraid of the devils. Now I love God and I am not afraid of the devils. I live very well.

"Maengamo, where is your son Kominkagi? Where is your son Ñamae? Why did you leave them behind? Why didn't you bring them? They will live well in the foreigners' house. Is your younger brother Dabu alive? Is your younger brother Kimo alive? They will live well with the foreigners. The foreigners will not be angry. They are very happy with the Aucas. If you keep spearing the foreigners, they are not angry in exchange. They just die, then they bury. Who killed the foreign man when they took Maruja? Who took her? Which of the Aucas came? Who speared? Tell me the truth. Why didn't you two call out and say, 'Don't spear! Come with us and visit. Here we two live.' Why did you let them come and kill? Why didn't you just come and get the machetes that the foreigners offered you?

"I lived with those same foreigners. They are like my relatives. I lived with them many moons. I went down the Napo and returned on the Curaray with them. When I was down there, I thought of all of you. I said, 'When will my relatives come? I don't know.' I went on downriver to the mouth of the Grape Tree River, and then upriver on the Grape Tree River. Four days I lived there thinking of you all. I said, 'When, oh when will my relatives come? Where is the trail? When will my little sister come? When will my big brother come? Do they live? I don't know.' I was right there on the trail, but I couldn't come to you.

"Visit well with the foreigners. When they come to your huts, do not spear them. The foreigners who love God are good foreigners. There are others who do not know God and drink fermented drink. But the foreigners who love God are very good.

"Who speared my uncle and my big brother? Maengamo, is your husband Gikita dead or alive? Does Umi's mother live? You didn't say anything about her. You just spoke about those who lived long ago. Talk to me straight and give me the answers. Tell me who lives. I know that my father died long ago.

"When I first came out of the forest, I lived in a foreigner's house. I just worked. I was hungry and hot. I said, 'When will I hear about God? I just live.'

"You live very well with a foreign woman. She does not understand the Auca speech. When she says, 'What is it? What is it?' you tell her what it is. Later she will understand.

"When you two came, another woman came with you. Then she ran away. Who was it who ran away? Tell me so that I will know. You say that your younger brother ran back into the forest. Was it Kimo or was it Dabu? Why didn't you call to him and say, 'Come with us'? Why did you let them run back into the forest? Don't be afraid. The foreigners won't kill you.

"Does Wiñaemi's mother live? Does Wiñaemi's older brother Nimonga live? Does Umi's sister Wiña live?"

Dayuma made a final desperate plea for information about the location of her family group. For over ten years she had heard nothing from her own people and wanted a truthful report about them.

"Whose hut did you two live in? How many of you lived there? Long ago we lived on Palm River. Later the foreigners came there and shot Omaenga, and she died. Then we lived on Fish River. Then Moipa did not do well and we fled. Now where do my people live? On what river do they live? You two speak to me. Do they live on Palm River, or on Fish River? I don't know. Where did you two live? Where were you living when you came out? When I heard that you two had come I had lots of fever and I could not go to you. That is all I speak."

February brought further breathtaking news. Betty Elliot had shown the two Auca women pictures from Palm Beach. While pointing to the woman nicknamed "Delilah," they had said "Imari." Betty relayed the word to Sulphur Springs.

"Gimari!" shouted Dayuma. "She is saying it is my sister Gimari!"

Dayuma had not recognized the pictures of "Delilah" as Gimari when Rachel showed them to her at Hacienda Ila. She was therefore elated at the news that Gimari was living at the time of Palm Beach—but was she still alive? So far the tapes had not mentioned either Gimari or her mother. And did Gimari's presence with her Aunt Mintaka at Palm Beach mean she was an orphan and her mother, Akawo, was dead?

As the weeks wore on with no word of them, Dayuma's patience wore thin. Rachel wrote Betty, "The girl is nearly crazy waiting to know if her mother still lives. She dreams almost every night that she and the two little sisters were speared. It is actually making her nervous to know that there is an answer available and she does not have it. She cries for her big brother—the tape gave all the details of his spearing and death. The smoldering fires of resentment would flare except for her desire to live as the Lord wants her to."

Finally, in late February, a tape brought the word for which Dayuma had wept and waited: Her mother, Akawo, was alive, and one daughter was living with her. But which daughter was it: Gimari or Oba? And had the other been killed? While Maengamo gave the welcome news about Akawo, Mintaka's voice was audible in the background: "Your mother is living like a wild pig alone in the forest, just eating squirrels that are blowgunned and fish from the streams."

Why was her mother living alone in the forest? Was she fleeing from spearings and had to live alone with no one to protect her? If she was eating squirrels, who blowgunned them for her? Dayuma concluded hopefully that her brother Nampa must be living with her mother and one sister in the forest.

The same tape brought more sad family news. Aunt Wiika and Aunt Wiwa had been speared by Moipa long ago.

"Now the trees have grown tall in the place where they were speared, and the wind blows in their branches," Maengamo reported mournfully.

But a final shock was yet in store for the Auca girl, whose spirit had been buffeted almost beyond endurance by the news of recent months. Rachel had sent Betty a picture of Dayuma with two toucan birds to be shown to Maengamo and Mintaka. Betty had set up two tape recorders—one to play Dayuma's questions, and the other to record the aunts' answers and comments on the picture.

When the picture of Dayuma was shown, Maengamo said, "You say this is her picture? She is dead!"

When it was pointed out that it was Dayuma's voice on the tape, they said, "Being dead she speaks."

The aunts had evaded the answers to many of Dayuma's questions. "Let her go herself and find out if she wants to know" was their impudent reply.

When Rachel had completed the translation of the last tape, she wrote Betty Elliot, "Someday perhaps we'll have some pleasant subject matter to work on without the deep emotional reaction that this stuff causes Dayuma. But maybe not until there is a quorum who love the Lord. A cross section of the material shows a fairly high percentage of spearing so far—in Dayuma's work as well as in that of these two."

Spearings had, in fact, dominated most of Maengamo's conversation. At one point she had blubbered out, "If your grandchildren grew up to be speared, and their grandchildren grew up to be speared, and their grandchildren grew up to be speared—you would cry, too!"

During the exchange of tapes, Betty Elliot wrote Rachel, "Maengamo's description of the murder of Moipa is a clear picture of the treachery of the people, isn't it? …Have you discovered what happened to Maengamo's husband? Or why her daughter died? Every time I ask about her husband, I get a reply full of spears and killings, so I have always assumed he was speared…."

Indeed, the tapes only confirmed what Rachel had learned through several years of language work with Dayuma: The Aucas were ruthless killers, not only on their borders, but also among themselves. The prospects for reaching the tribe were, in one sense, darker than ever.

# CHAPTER THIRTEEN

# What Doth Hinder Me...?

For months Dayuma had been praying that her eight-year-old son in Ecuador might join her in the States. She longed for him.

When Rachel and Dayuma left the hacienda for the television program, they had expected to be gone only a month. Efforts had since been made to arrange the trip of the young boy to join his mother. Now the thrill of Sulphur Springs' first snow reminded Dayuma of him again. How she would enjoy sharing this experience with her son! But as the weeks wore on and the child did not appear, the possibility of snow during his arrival grew slim. Dayuma added to her daily prayers for the lad's coming an earnest petition for the snow to last longer.

"The Lord *must* answer her prayers for her boy—they are so spontaneous and precious!" Rachel wrote fellow workers in Ecuador, who were trying to obtain the documents necessary for his departure.

Dayuma, of course, could not understand all the paperwork involved before the boy could leave Ecuador. Her impatience grew when the many phone calls and letters about her son brought no results. Then one day Captain Larry Montgomery of Wycliffe's Jungle Aviation and Radio Service (JAARS) landed on a small field near Sulphur Springs.When Dayuma heard that he was headed for Ecuador, she went to Montgomery with a special commission. When he got to Ecuador, would he please get her small son and bring him to her as soon as possible? The Indian girl, accustomed to delivering messages orally in the jungle, had more confidence in a personal arrangement with a JAARS pilot than in the prolific exchange of letters, which had accomplished nothing.

Rachel was surprised at the request. Within two weeks, however, man-of-action Montgomery telephoned from Miami that he had just arrived by plane and had the small boy in tow. At the airport in Tulsa, Oklahoma, mother and son were finally reunited. In his report of aviation activities for the month, Montgomery included "delivery of small boy."

"I always knew that our JAARS fellows would willingly do many things for us beyond the line of duty," Rachel remembers, "but I hadn't expected he would be able to carry out Dayuma's special commission so successfully."

Dayuma's prayer for snow was also answered with abundance. This time Rachel dressed her two jungle Indians in warm clothes to sled and make snowballs and snowmen to their hearts' content. Of this event, Rachel wrote to friends in Sulphur Springs, "Perhaps you folks didn't know why there was so much snow so late in the season. We think it was because a young Indian mother asked the Lord to send the marvelous 'white' once more after her son arrived. So He sent three more snows in two weeks in early March!"

But there was something even more important to Dayuma than snow for her son, who was now being called "Sammy" by his American playmates. On the very first day of his arrival, the joyful mother began to relate the wonders of God and His Son, Jesus. The wide-eyed boy drank in the stories with as much eagerness as the mother poured them out. In three sessions on their first Sunday together, amounting to about three and a half hours, Dayuma told her son all she had learned about God and Jesus during the months she had been separated from him.

Nor did her ardor cool. Each day she continued to teach Sammy in minute detail what she was learning from Rachel. The months of patient work with Dayuma had not been lost.

Sammy's presence was a balm for Dayuma, who had passed through a dark valley, shadowed by death itself. Transparent joy in imparting her knowledge of the Lord to him was unmistakable evidence of her refreshed spirit.

Before Sammy arrived, Rachel had questioned Dayuma, "If your son asks you what will happen when he dies, what will you tell him?"

"I'll tell him," Dayuma had answered, " 'if you die first, and go to God's house in heaven, I will come later and see you again. And if I die first, I will go to heaven, and you will come later, and I will see you again.' " Then, remembering her old Auca teaching about the termite, she added, "Having gone to heaven, you will not die again!"

As Sammy heard of heaven by day and by night, Dayuma began to think concretely about transmitting the wonders of God's carving to her own people in the forest. "If I go to the Auca huts, what will they say? What will they do?" she queried. She had been away from her relatives for so long that she faced the possibility of not being accepted. One day she said determinedly to Rachel, "I'll go back—don't you go. If they are angry at me, I will die."

With her thoughts turned southward toward Mintaka and Maengamo and her tribe, Dayuma wondered how she might tell them the story. Perhaps the words of Grandfather's old song about "God created everything" might be applied to the Bible story of creation. She prayed that her people would not reject her message, but that they would believe God's carving.

As news came from Señor Sevilla that Dayuma and her son were being released to Rachel for the Auca work, the girl seemed concerned. She asked, "Who will feed us if we do not go back to the patrón?"

"We belong to the Lord and serve Him," Rachel told her, "and He will provide food for us. We will ask Him, and He will supply."

It was a long step of faith for the girl, who had worked from sunrise to sunset in the field in exchange for food for herself and her little boy. Rachel saw that the girl was now ready to face the uncertainties of the future, including the dubious reception by her own group. They began to make plans for the trip homeward.

During the day, Rachel analyzed the Auca texts. But not knowing when, if ever, she would have the same opportunity for teaching Dayuma the Word, she also spent many hours with her, reviewing the lessons taught and covering new ground. One night as she was teaching her the narrative of the baptism of Jesus, Rachel noticed unusual interest. Dayuma listened carefully to all the details, and then repeated the story. Her interest was so great that Rachel cited two other examples of Bible baptism: the Philippian jailer who was baptized following his remarkable conversion, and the Ethiopian eunuch who asked to be baptized. Dayuma was impressed with the words of the eunuch: "Here is water. What doth hinder me to be baptized?" She fixed all the facts of the stories in her mind, and retold them practically word for word in her own language.

Fully two weeks later, Dayuma startled Rachel with the question, "What good man of God can enter me into the water?"

Rachel had not expected the request so soon. She had thought that sometime, in Ecuador, the girl would be baptized. But the serious question and the earnest desire of the girl challenged Rachel into unanticipated action. As she prayed about "what good man of God" would understand the circumstances and perform a meaningful ceremony, she remembered Dr. Edman's vital interest in the girl from the first days of language work on the hacienda in 1955. One Christmas in Ecuador, Dayuma had met Dr. and Mrs. Edman in the Larson home. They had been most gracious to the strange Indian girl. As a personal friend, he would surely be willing to have a quiet, private baptismal service for Dayuma. Rachel knew that his son lived near Sulphur Springs. Perhaps on a visit to Arkansas, Dr. Edman could perform the ceremony. She wrote him a note at Wheaton College and was amazed at the plan he suggested in reply:

"My heart was deeply stirred, Rachel, at your report of the tape that has gone from Dayuma to Mintaka and Maengamo, the first Auca testimony for the Lord Jesus in her own language to her own people. I shall be sharing this word with the whole College family, so we shall be trusting earnestly with you.

"My heart was likewise deeply stirred by the word of invitation to have her baptism. We shall be looking upward for the Lord's guidance and provision in that regard. It seemed to me there might be the possibility in the Lord's good will that the LeTourneaus bring Dayuma here some spring day, either a weekday or on a weekend; and we could have the baptismal service here. It would be most appropriate, it seems to me, to have the baptism in Wheaton, from which three of the five martyrs went on their way toward the gates of splendor. I shall be checking with the folk in Texas with recommendation for a date in May or April when the weather is warmer. (Our thermometer read 12 below this morning at daybreak!)

"Little by little the story of the past is being unraveled; and the pages of the future grow more exciting and wonderful!"

Rachel answered, "You folks take my breath away! I had thought only of a baptism near here somewhere, and presto!..." She concluded the letter, giving consent to Dr. Edman's plan with the words, "Someday there will be other Aucas saying, 'See, here is the Curaray. What doth hinder us to be baptized?'"

The service was to be held in Wheaton on April 15, and industrialist R. G. LeTourneau agreed to pick up the trio in his private plane in Sulphur Springs. Very full days of packing and preparation preceded the big event. The baptismal service would mark the initial step in the homeward journey for the first Auca missionary to her own tribe.

Rachel learned in Wheaton that the ceremony had been publicly announced. It was consummated as planned on April 15 in the Wheaton Evangelical Free Church, pastored by Wilbur Nelson, Marj Saint's former pastor from California. Three languages—Auca, English, and Spanish—were used in the service in a thrilling review of how "Christianity came to the first member of one of the last Stone Age tribes in existence." Rachel had regretted that there was insufficient time to notify friends who would have had a special interest in the occasion. She had thought of the Larsons, the pioneers to the Oriente in Ecuador. She knew that they were in the States, but did not know where. It was a delight, therefore, when Rachel found they had been notified and were present. Mr. and Mrs. Fred Elliot, parents of Jim Elliot, attended, as well as his sister,

Mrs. Jane Hawthorne. Mrs. T. E. McCulley, mother of Ed McCulley, was also there. Wycliffe was represented by Dr. Richard Pittman, deputy director, who accompanied the party in LeTourneau's plane.

Dr. Carl Amerding, professor of Bible at Wheaton and former missionary to South America, delivered the message. "I know of nothing else in my experience that compares to this," he said in a moving evaluation of the significance of the occasion. Then, as a stirring climax, Dr. Edman, the "good man of God," baptized Dayuma in a simple act of immersion as the first Auca Christian, smiling radiantly, gave witness to her faith in Christ. Sammy was dedicated to the Lord by his mother before her baptism. She hoped that he, too, would follow the Lord all the days of his life.

From Wheaton, the Auca party traveled to the East Coast for a farewell visit with the Saint family and to arrange documents for their departure. That the preparations for the return to Ecuador would require some delay was beyond Dayuma's comprehension. Finally, by the end of May, they were guests of Sam Saint and Cornell Capa in the Gold Room at Idlewild Airport, where thick steaks were served on gold plates. Later, when asked what Dayuma thought of the gold plates, Rachel replied, "The Aucas know nothing of the value of gold. The girl thought a lot more of the big juicy steaks *on* the plates."

Rachel, Dayuma, and Sammy left New York City early one morning and the next day were at Limoncocha, Wycliffe's base in the heart of the Ecuadorian jungle. The return trip had been as breathtaking as the sudden flight to California the year before.

As they flew over the Napo River from Shell Mera to Limoncocha, Dayuma looked down on Auca territory she had not seen since she fled from her home so many years before. Rachel was amazed that as Dayuma studied the lay of the land, she remembered the name of each river and ridge.

"Over there is where they killed my grandfather," she said, pointing to a ridge in the east. It was all very familiar. This country was home to the Auca girl.

Within a few minutes, they would be landing at the jungle base. There Betty Elliot with Mintaka and Maengamo would join them! "Will my aunts recognize me?" wondered Dayuma.

She had recently dreamed that they thought she was a foreigner.

# CHAPTER FOURTEEN

# Hope Springs Eternal in a Mother's Breast

In a secluded corner of Limoncocha Base, a small Auca clearing was readied for Mintaka and Maengamo. Dayuma knew what would make them feel at home, and had given some welcome suggestions to the Wycliffe personnel who were preparing for the big event. Quichua workmen hurriedly constructed palm-thatched shelters where the Auca women could make their customary ground fires. Dayuma and Rachel hung hammocks from the posts of the shelters overlooking the placid lake where Dayuma herself planned to go spear-fishing with them. An Indian had been sent to the forest to hunt the wild game that abounded. Succulent yuca grew plentifully in the jungle garden in another clearing connected by a shaded trail.

Rachel was almost as charged with anticipation as Dayuma.

"What shall I say to your aunts?" she asked, planning a greeting in Auca. "Shall I say, 'I like you'?"

"No!" Dayuma replied with vigor. "You say, 'I'm not angry with you!'"

Dayuma began orienting Rachel on how to receive her aunts and put them at ease. She selected for Rachel the Auca name "Nimu," meaning "Star." It had been the name of Dayuma's little sister who was hacked to death by Moipa's machete. One point of instruction was emphasized: Rachel was not to ask about the circumstances of Palm Beach until the aunts became well acquainted with her. They might think she was planning to avenge her pilot brother's death.

Suddenly, word flashed over the radio that the plane bearing Betty Elliot and the two Auca women had left Shandia and would be landing at Limoncocha in half an hour. Dayuma immediately went to the airstrip and began to watch the clear blue sky above the giant trees. She paced up and down the narrow strip, which ran between walls of towering jungle from which it had been cut.

Dayuma's heart pounded, and she rubbed her hands nervously as a distant speck growing larger and humming loudly moved toward her. Soon the plane was on the grassy strip, taxiing right for her. As the craft neared, Dayuma saw her two aunts, and her eyes filled with tears. She was trembling with emotion. Before the plane stopped moving, Mintaka pressed her face against the glass and shouted, "Dayuma! Dayuma!" Maengamo recognized her instantly, too, and was talking and gesturing wildly when the door of the plane opened. The two women tumbled out talking, especially Maengamo. In almost hysterically fast Auca she was continuing the harangue, begun on the tapes, about Moipa and the spearings which had thinned out Dayuma's family group during the last eleven years.

"They speared your brother Wawae..." were almost the first words that greeted Dayuma. In the burning midday sun at the door of the plane, Maengamo poured out the details of Dayuma's brother's death.

"It's hot here in the sun—let's go—" It was Mintaka who finally interrupted the recital of family spearings.

Rachel moved the knot of Auca speakers into the shade of the airplane wing. But Maengamo continued to go over and over the sad story. Dayuma had heard most of it on tape, but getting it first-hand, face-to-face with her aunts, was too much for her. She turned around, buried her face in her handkerchief, and wept. By this time a curious crowd of Quichua Indian workers had gathered.

Rachel's heart ached for Dayuma. She suggested that they go to their house and continue talking there. The three Aucas settled quickly and naturally in their wooded dwelling area. Dayuma felt they might tell the truth only to her, so at first they were left alone to talk over the long years of family history since they had last seen one another. Around the fire they ate roasted bananas, yuca, and fresh fish, while talking incessantly.

Rachel made her headquarters in a bamboo and chonta palm cabin, while Betty Elliot and her little daughter, Valerie, settled temporarily in another. At night, Dayuma slept in Rachel's quarters and reported on the events of the day. She was hearing a great deal of family news—some of it good, but most of it punctuated with spears.

Rachel later hung her hammock under a thatched roof adjoining the Auca shelter where she could hear the fast nasal language as it continued all day and far into the night. Under her mosquito net at night, she listened to questions and answers weaving the intricate design of the Auca way of life predominated by revenge spearings. One night, Rachel heard the aunts tell Dayuma of spearing after spearing. When a killer was named, Dayuma would ask, "And then who speared him in exchange?" Retaliation…spearings back and forth…always avenging the death of a relative. For more than a solid hour of "Who speared in exchange?" Dayuma absorbed another tragic chapter of family history.

Uppermost in Dayuma's mind were questions about her mother: Where did she live? With whom did she live? This vital information should be had soon, in case Maengamo and Mintaka suddenly disappeared. It required many days of talking and eating around the ground fire for the full story to unfold. Maengamo was not given to logical narration. Essential facts about her family were often revealed to Dayuma as incidentals in the incessant flow of unordered sequence emanating from Maengamo. Eventually, by piecing the bits together, Dayuma learned the fate of all her family.

In the first days around the fire, she found that Maengamo had left three of her children with Dayuma's mother. Mintaka's son was also living with her.

After Dayuma fled the forest, the family had gradually migrated downriver, deep into the jungle and far from the outside world. It was so far in the interior that it took them two months of river travel and walking on jungle trail to get back to their former location. By the time Maengamo and Mintaka left the forest, the family had returned and were living almost as near the outside as they had ever been. It was only a few days to Dayuma's mother's hut.

Dayuma recognized the hand of God in moving her family to an accessible place. If they had still been living in the deep jungle, it would have been almost impossible to locate them. Rachel, too, saw the providential significance of the present location, for it was this new site that her brother Nate had spotted from the air. Preceding the contact with Dayuma's family at Palm Beach, he had dropped gifts from the plane into the clearing. The knowledge that her mother was living nearby stimulated Dayuma's desire to return to her family.

Despite her anxiety to solve all the family enigmas, Dayuma could not resist the urge to communicate the wonder of God's carving to her aunts. Between the mouthfuls of delicious fresh-caught fish and gulps of banana drink, Dayuma regaled her aunts with bits of biblical information utterly foreign to them. Although they were skeptical, the natural-born narrator held them spellbound by the abundant and fresh supply of Bible history which she had stored up, and which now overflowed.

"God lives high in the sky," she said. "He is the One who will never die…. Tariri used to say that the boa was God, but now he knows God…." Dayuma drew from her acquaintance with the converted Shapra chief to emphasize her teaching about God. And, of course, she was desirous of making heaven as attractive as possible to her relatives. There would be no gnats in heaven—no bites to scratch. "And there we will not grow old and die. And we will never be hungry in God's house high up in the sky—"

Maengamo looked doubtful. Then, craning her neck and looking up to the clear sky beyond the thatch, she asked, "What will we eat in God's house? There's no yuca growing up there!" Food in quantity—yes, it was a chief preoccupation of all Aucas. Maengamo was not one to accept new information without question. She was a challenge to an alert teacher struggling to plant intangible, eternal facts in virgin soil.

Rachel occasionally joined Dayuma in the attempt to teach her aunts. One day when it was storming, Rachel noticed that Mintaka was burning a thick wad of beeswax. The Auca woman was thus trying to avert the disaster of big trees blowing down on her flimsy shelter.

"Why don't you talk to God who created the wind?" Rachel asked her.

Talking to God was a new idea. Mintaka was struck by the thought.

"Talk to God? How do you talk to God—like this—?" and Mintaka stood up dramatically, threw her arms outward, turned her face toward the sky, and began addressing God in fast Auca. Rachel turned her head slightly to conceal a surprised smile. She had been unable to guess what Mintaka's reaction to this new teaching would be, except that it would be refreshingly uninhibited.

Dayuma was a match for the unpredictable relatives. To Rachel's amazement, Bible narratives always came out in typical Auca settings, in characteristic Auca style. Dayuma applied the graphic storytelling technique used in tales of spearings.

One day, Dayuma was describing an imaginary scene in heaven.

"Who comes now?" a voice says in heaven as someone approaches.

"Her name is Maengamo."

"She believed very well?...who are *you?*"

"Mintaka."

"All right. Come on in. Here I have thatched your hut."

When the truth was presented too graphically for immediate acceptance and the aunts wore quizzical expressions, Dayuma would comment, "I don't just say this myself. God speaks it!" She always made it plain that the source of her amazing information was God's carving.

One day as she was urging her aunts to receive pardon offered through God's Son, she challenged them with the question, "Whose heart will become like light?" Rachel was puzzled as to the precise Bible passage that prompted the question, but she thought it was a good idea.

The story of Noah and the ark pictured God in an animated conversation with Noah.

" 'Now when you finish building it, let me know,' God said to Noah…. Then when the people were all dead, it stopped raining." Daniel in the "jaguars'" den was a real thriller, even to Rachel who had heard the account many times. With gestures, spellbinding voice changes, and realistic sound effects produced by the gift of mimicry, Dayuma created suspense and excitement as the aunts heard about Daniel for the first time. When the king, who wondered if Daniel were still alive, called down into the den, he heard the familiar Auca answer: "Oo—oo—!" as the storyteller imitated the response to a jungle call.

Dayuma tried to impress the aunts with God's power. He is the One who rules over everything in the world. He speaks, and all of nature obeys. "If God speaks, the rain doesn't rain," she told them. "In stilling the storm on the big water, He said to the wind, 'Why do you blow?' And the wind heard."

Even the parable of the fig tree came eloquently to life with Dayuma's colorful touch. "Jesus said to the barren tree, 'Why do you not bear seeds? You are just selfish. You will die!'"

Sometimes Rachel wondered just how far she would let the girl's interpolation go without some slight correction. One day when telling the story of the crucifixion, Dayuma said that "the sun stopped shining and the day became like night so that God couldn't see them hitting His Son."

As Dayuma shared her knowledge of God with her aunts, she was sharply reminded that her people had no basis for understanding this completely new truth. She knew it would take time—and patient teaching—to convince them. She thought of others in her family and wondered how they would respond to stories Grandfather had never heard.

Her mother, Akawo, still lived, and quite near the outside world. Dayuma began to relive old scenes in the forest as her aunts reminded her of home. She wondered about her mother's attitude toward her, remembering with a twinge of pain that Akawo had once threatened to strangle her. And there was no fond father to return to now.

"Does my mother want to see me?" Dayuma wondered.

"Of course she wants to see you!" exclaimed the aunts in unison. "She's been looking for you ever since you left!"

Dayuma looked at them incredulously.

"Your mother begged us to look for you and bring you home if we found you," assured Maengamo. "She said she would bring a whole mess of fish, and we will have a feast."

"Yes!" Mintaka continued. "She told us to look for you at the foreigners' houses. She said that if you were married and your husband wouldn't let you come, she would understand—but she wants you to come home. 'If she is a widow and has children, tell her to come and bring the children.' That's what your mother told me to tell you."

Then her aunts, sometimes both talking at once, described in detail her mother's search for her down through the years. With no evidence that Dayuma lived, but with an undying desire to see her again, she had never given up hope of her daughter's return. She commissioned Ominia, and Tyaenyae, Wiñaemi's mother, to find her. Ominia and little Wiñaemi had gone to the outside world and never returned, but Tyaenyae had retreated, frightened by the foreigners' guns.

"Tyaenyae came back and told us that the foreigners had probably killed Ominia and Wiñaemi—and had surely killed you, too," said Mintaka, recollecting the sadness of her sister Akawo when Tyaenyae had returned with only bad news.

"But I am alive—and Ominia and Wiñaemi still live at the patrón's house!" cried Dayuma.

"Yes, but Akawo doesn't know it," Maengamo replied. "She just lives out in the forest and knows nothing about those who have fled. We must go home and tell her."

"Your mother waited and looked for you for many moons after Tyaenyae returned," continued Mintaka. "Then one day she said that she herself would go to the outside and look for you. She said that she would take Gimari and Oba—they were still little children then—and look for you."

"But my husband, Gikita, wouldn't let her go!" exclaimed Maengamo. "He said, 'No, I will not let you go. You and the children would surely die.'"

Dayuma looked from one aunt to the other, hardly daring to believe it. Her mother, in spite of her great fear of the foreigners, had tried to search for her. And dear old Uncle Gikita had been caring for her mother after her father, Tyaento, was speared.

"Many more moons passed," the aunts continued, "but your mother would not believe that you were dead."

It was Maengamo who reminisced and reconstructed with Mintaka's help all the details of another search for the missing girl.

"Then one day your mother said to your brother Wawae, 'Go look for your sister Dayuma. Go to the foreigners and look until you find some sign or word from her. I must know about my Dayuma.'

"My brother Kimo went with Wawae to look for you—he was just a young boy then. Wawae and Kimo went through the forest until they saw a big trail that the foreigners had cut. Then they saw a foreign man. Kimo was afraid and ran and hid in the trees. Wawae, unafraid at first, began talking to the foreigner. Being afraid of the Auca man, the foreigner cried out and ran, too."

At that point in the story, the two aunts and Dayuma laughed heartily.

"But Wawae stayed there and called and called," Maengamo resumed. "Finally, the foreigner returned with a gift of a new machete. Wawae took only the workman's own small broken one. He was afraid that Moipa or someone else would kill him to get the other.

"Then Wawae asked the foreigner where you and the others lived on the outside. Where? and Where? and Where do they live? he kept saying. But the foreigner didn't understand.

"Then several foreigners saw Kimo hiding in the forest, and they were very afraid! But Wawae said, 'He's only a child,' and he called him to come out. Wawae wanted to go with the foreigners, but they only pointed to the trail back into the forest. They wouldn't take Wawae and Kimo with them.

"As they sadly started home, there on the big trail some Quichuas came carrying loads. But when they saw Wawae and Kimo, they dropped their loads and ran.

"Wawae and Kimo wanted to see the foreigners' possessions, so they hid in the forest and waited. But two other foreigners came with guns and took all their possessions away. Returning, Wawae and Kimo told your mother that you were surely dead."

As Dayuma heard the story, she told her aunts the other side of the incident which she had heard at Hacienda Ila. The Quichuas who had fled were carriers for the Shell Oil Company, which was prospecting in the area. They had come to the settlement on the Curaray, shaken and frightened at the sight of the Aucas they encountered on the trail.

"They said they stored all their things in an Auca hut," Dayuma related.

"Yes, the hut was very full," added Maengamo. "And our men said, 'We must not take anything.' There were lots of foreigners, and they might shoot us with their guns." For a long time they didn't return, and we said perhaps they left things for us. Then they came back and took everything except two axes, foreigners' fire sticks, and machetes, and we said, 'Yes, now this is what they left for us'—and we took them."

The three Aucas enjoyed the joke as the story of Wawae was matched by the foreigners' side of the tale. Dayuma's laughter soon turned to tears, however, as Maengamo suddenly shifted the scene.

"Poor Wawae! Now he is dead—!" and she recounted how other Aucas, whom he thought had come on a friendly visit, speared him in his hut instead.

"Our people fled and then returned to bury him, but they dug up his body and speared him again."

Weeping, Dayuma went to find Rachel.

"What is it, Dayuma?" asked Rachel. "Is it your mother? Is your mother dead?"

"No, she lives"—but the girl continued to weep violently. "It is my big brother—"

"But, Dayuma, you already knew that he was dead."

"I know—but they dug up his body—"

"But haven't I told you that it doesn't matter what happens to the body?"

"Yes—I know that—but my big brother didn't know the Lord, and his soul didn't go up to God's house in heaven!" Her body heaved with heavy sobs.

"At that point I wept with her," Rachel says. "I dreaded the day when the question about relatives who had never heard would come up, and this was the day. It was an agonizing heart cry of the first one in the Auca tribe to know the Lord."

Rachel was quick to remind the weeping girl that God had spared her mother and others of her family. Perhaps she would be the only one who could safely return to tell those who still lived about the Lord Jesus.

The next day Dayuma heard another installment of her mother's unceasing search for her.

Dayuma's half brother Minkayi had escaped the spearings that took Wawae's life, and was determined to flee to the outside world. He promised Akawo he would look for Dayuma. For several days he went downriver, looking for a place where he had heard many foreigners lived. He finally arrived at their big house, where they received him kindly.

Minkayi would go blowgunning in the forest and bring back meat, which he shared with the foreigners. But the foreigners did not reciprocate. One day when they shot a tapir, only a small piece was offered to Minkayi. Hungry and very angry, he watched the foreigners consume the meat. Shortly, he left and returned to his forest home.

He decided to settle the injustice. Before long the spears were ready, and an armed expedition of reprisal went to the offending foreigners. The Aucas waited for them to come within spearing distance. Soon they heard voices nearby and saw people moving among the trees. Amid savage shouts of anger, the spears flew through the air toward the targets. Minkayi heard a startled scream and a muffled groan. Through the trees he saw two figures fall.

As the spearmen retreated into the forest, they heard the buzzing of the foreigners' wood-bee overhead. It came closer, circled over them, and swooped down near the place where the spears had struck. Then the buzzing stopped. The big bee had come down to rest on the very spot! As Minkayi and his companions continued their journey into the forest, they heard the loud buzzing again. Had the foreigners' wood-bee, like the buzzard, so quickly discovered the speared victims?

As Dayuma listened, she questioned Maengamo and Mintaka further. What rivers had Minkayi followed? Where had he seen the foreigners? How long ago had this happened? As she heard the facts, she began to make her own calculations. Yes, it was to the Quichuas at the army post of Villano that Minkayi had come. And she knew about the Indian man and woman who had been speared. So it was Minkayi!

But Dayuma knew something more. It was Rachel's younger brother Nate who flew the foreigners' wood-bee and who happened to be near the spot when the spears struck. And it was her brother who had flown the wounded Quichua woman to Shell Mera with a spear tip lodged in her spine.

Dayuma looked thoughtfully into the fire as her aunts continued their long, involved story of a mother's relentless search for a missing daughter.

⟋↷ ⟋↷ ⟋↷ ⟋↷

After Minkayi's failure to find Dayuma, there was more discussion around the Auca fires at night out in the isolated forest. Reports concerning foreigners had been unfavorable. They were stingy—and inhospitable. And more than likely, the Aucas who had found their way to the outside and never returned were eaten by them. Yes, the outsiders were cannibals after all. Where was Dayuma? There had been no word of her for more than seven years now.

With a sigh, Akawo admitted that it must have been so with Dayuma—but with no actual evidence, she still wondered.

Akawo's daughter Gimari, who had miraculously escaped death in the big storm before Dayuma left the forest, was of marriageable age. She was maturing rapidly. Akawo planned that she would marry Dyuwi, a strong young man who was a suitable match for her attractive daughter. Oba, Akawo's younger daughter, was still enjoying a carefree, happy girlhood in the forest.

Akawo's young son Nampa, whom Dayuma had thrown clear of falling trees in the storm, was now a young man. He was old enough to know that he was a likely target for the spears of Naenkiwi, Moipa's successor. Naenkiwi had now mastered the technique skillfully used for many years by his teacher. His threats to other Aucas who would not follow his plans of attack generated the same terrifying power unleashed by Moipa. He was widely feared, and hated by many.

Like Moipa, Naenkiwi had taken several wives—to the consternation of the younger men soon to become eligible husbands. He had forcibly abducted his first wife after spearing her father. He had carried off his second young wife, still in early adolescence, from the home of her protesting brother. In a fit of fury he had spear-killed his first wife. Looking for still another, he had decided on Gimari.

As soon as Naenkiwi showed interest in her young daughter, Akawo protested. He would not snatch Gimari away! But Naenkiwi had set his heart on the girl and was not to be refused. The determined suitor had made his plans.

Naenkiwi had arranged a traditional wedding party, where he would take Gimari as his bride. At the all-night dance, the guests would place him and Gimari together in a hammock, thus signifying they were man and wife.

But Akawo, suddenly realizing what was going to happen at the party, grabbed Gimari by the hand and said, "Let's go"—and they fled into the forest. They built a shelter and stayed there all night. Late the next day they returned to the clearing.

Naenkiwi was furious. He came again for Gimari, sputtering threats to spear Akawo and Nampa if they wouldn't let her marry him. Again they said, "No!" and Naenkiwi was really angry.

Meanwhile, Naenkiwi had won Gimari's heart. During the days of conflict, she had become blindly infatuated with her persistent lover and wanted to become his wife. He continued to press his claims, now aided by Gimari herself.

There was also other excitement in those days. A foreigners' wood-bee that began to buzz overhead would sometimes swoop low over Akawo's clearing, make loud noises, and drop foreigners' things from a vine hanging from its insides. One day as Nampa watched the wood-bee circling overhead, he saw a shining object coming down in front of his hut. It was a foreigners' pot, and it dropped right at his feet. Another day he watched as the vine dropped a strange bundle in front of him. In it he found a new kind of foreigners' birds—small winged creatures that had never appeared in the forest. He fed them daily and proudly raised the foreigners' pets.

"If the wood-bee comes again, I am going to send a parrot in exchange," said Nampa. Carefully, he wrapped the jungle bird in a housing of bark cloth and fed it bits of banana. He began counting the days, and when he had used all the fingers on one hand and two on the other, the buzzing bee came again and swooped low over the clearing. He tied the parrot to the long vine hanging from the bee circling overhead. Then up went the big bee with the parrot.

Many times afterward the wood-bee came and dropped good and useful gifts in Nampa's clearing. Surely, thought the Aucas, there were other Aucas up there in the sky, sending down the gifts! "Who but Aucas would give us such nice things?" they reasoned.

And could it be that Dayuma herself—if perchance she lived— was giving good things to her very own family? Perhaps she was trying to say, "I am alive! I remember my mother, and my brothers, and my sisters!"

The possibility stimulated Akawo.

Nampa, too, felt that the wood-bee knew something about his sister Dayuma.

"The next time it flies overhead, I am going to climb the vine and go find Dayuma," he announced one day.

"Don't go! You would only be killed," Akawo said. But when the wood-bee came again and dropped its vine, Nampa ran to the bamboo platform he had made for climbing to the bee. Then clutching the vine, he started up toward the circling wood-bee. With a sudden snap the vine broke, and Nampa went tumbling down to the platform in great disappointment.

"Now when will I find Dayuma?" he asked sadly as the foreigners' wood-bee flew off without him.

The visits of the big bee were the talk of the forest. Speculation ran high as the animated Aucas spoke far into the night around the fires. And hope revived in Akawo as she connected the buzzing creature with her long-lost daughter. It had dropped a piece of wood with five nicks carved on it. That was sure proof! Dayuma was sending a message to her family. Umi, Ominia, Winaemi, Aepi, and Dayuma must be alive. Perhaps she was saying, "Come! Come to me on the outside!" Old Akawo's imagination soared.

One day as several men from the clearing were hunting in the forest near the Curaray, they heard the sound of chopping in the distance. It was like the noise of a big woodpecker hard at work. They followed the sound through the trees, out to the beach by the Curaray. They crept closer and peered between the big trunks.

There before their unbelieving eyes they saw the foreigners' wood-bee resting on the sand, and several foreigners chopping wood busily. Shocked by the unusual sight, they hurried back to the clearing to share the news. What could it mean? Did the foreigners bring word from Dayuma?

Around the fire that night as the frogs croaked and the crickets chirped, all the Aucas in the clearing talked at once in loud, excited tones. A plan was forming in Akawo's mind.

"Why don't you go to the foreigners on the beach and ask them to take you to Dayuma?" she asked Gimari, her eyes bright with excitement. Mintaka would go along with her.

The idea appealed to Gimari. It was a possible escape from her dilemma. She wanted to marry Naenkiwi, but not at the cost of her mother and brother's lives.

"Nampa and I will come later," Akawo proposed. "If the foreigners are not angry, you call us, and we will go with you."

There was little sleep that night as preparations were made for the trip to the Curaray. At daybreak Gimari and her Aunt Mintaka were on the trail. A short distance through the forest, they heard someone coming toward them. It was Naenkiwi, who had learned of the plan and was determined that Gimari would not escape. He joined the two women.

As they reached the river's edge, they heard the sound of chopping. Curiously, they peered through the trees, and saw that the foreigners had built a small shelter and were still chopping wood.

"Let's cross the river," suggested Gimari. But Naenkiwi hesitated. He wondered if the foreigners had guns.

"I'm going," said Gimari, and with that she was in the water, wading toward the sandy beach. Mintaka and Naenkiwi followed.

"Gimari wants to go with you in your wood-bee," said Naenkiwi as he approached the foreigners. "She is Dayuma's sister."

"Take me to my sister Dayuma," pleaded Gimari.

"I want to go, too," added Mintaka.

But the foreigners did not understand. They took Naenkiwi alone up in the bee, circled around over Akawo's clearing, and came back to the beach. Still they failed to understand that Gimari wanted to go where Dayuma lived. The hours wore on and the mission was unsuccessful. The sun was sinking below the big trees.

"Dayuma is dead!" Gimari said in sudden disappointment. "That's why they don't want to take me!"

"They have killed and eaten Dayuma and the other Aucas. They will kill you, too," Naenkiwi added, ordering Gimari to leave.

Angry and disheartened, she turned around, waded across the river, and started through the forest followed by Naenkiwi. But Mintaka lingered with the foreigners.

As Naenkiwi and Gimari returned on the trail, they met Akawo and Nampa, with Dayuma's younger sisters Oba and Ana. They were planning to join Gimari as promised. Their old axes had been thrown away since they were expecting to receive new ones from the foreigners. Naenkiwi, however, gave them a bad report concerning the foreigners.

"They would only kill you," he told them, ordering the little family group to go home. "They tried to kill us."

When Akawo and her children arrived back at the clearing, she found everyone preparing to follow her and go with the foreigners. She relayed Naenkiwi's news.

"How do they know that they are *bad* foreigners?" Maengamo challenged Akawo. "They couldn't understand what the foreigners were saying. They are young. I am older. I will join Mintaka on the Curaray and see for myself!"

Naenkiwi and Gimari arrived at dusk. The village was quiet. All had gone to rest in their hammocks, and Gimari slipped quietly into her hut. Naenkiwi was still bent on taking Gimari. Silently, he entered his hut, picked up his spears and, machete in hand, crept stealthily to Gikita's hut.

His sister Miñimo, who had discovered his plan, followed him secretly. As Naenkiwi lifted his spear to kill first Gikita and then Nampa, Miñimo grabbed him by the throat from behind and started to scream.

"Flee—all of you—run fast!" she called. Gimari's cousin Nimonga sprang quickly to his feet and grabbed Naenkiwi from behind while Gikita held him in front. The other men took his spears and broke them and stole his machetes.

"Why do you spear?" Nampa shouted angrily. "Why don't you just ask for Gimari and not kill to get her? Now take her and go!"

Akawo objected. "No! You cannot take her!" And she grabbed her daughter.

But Nampa snatched Gimari away and gave her to Naenkiwi. "Now take her and go to the foreigners and live!"

"I will not go to the foreigners," protested Naenkiwi. "They would only kill us. They have killed Dayuma and the other four girls. They are *bad* foreigners and will kill the rest of us Aucas. They beat us and tried to kill us with machetes."

"I am going anyway!" exclaimed Maengamo. She had already made preparations for the trip.

"If you do, I will go myself and kill the foreigners," threatened Naenkiwi.

While the argument continued, Naenkiwi took Gimari and started off through the forest.

"Don't ever come back to us!"Akawo shouted furiously after them.

Naenkiwi's report was discussed by the men in the clearing. They became convinced that the foreigners had killed Dayuma and the other four. They were angry.

"Tomorrow we will go and see for ourselves!" they declared.

But the next morning, Mintaka returned and reported on her visit.

"They were good foreigners!" she said enthusiastically. "They laughed a lot!"

"But Naenkiwi said they were bad—they tried to kill you," protested some of her listeners.

"He lied!" shouted Mintaka. "They didn't try to kill us—they were good to us!"

But Gimari had agreed with Naenkiwi, and the men were already making spears.

"If we don't kill them, they will surely kill us," someone suggested. And all the ill treatment of the tribe at the hand of the foreigners was carefully reviewed.

"Yes, they will kill us and eat us," another added.

"There are only five of them now, but more may come. They might kill us all."

The majority decided to stop them before they killed more Aucas.

"Let's make lots of spears fast!" Minkayi urged. The men began working feverishly. By the next morning, they were in a savage frenzy.

"Let's go!" commanded Gitika finally.

Raging and yelling, they set off at dawn for the Curaray.

✍ ✍ ✍ ✍

"They spear-killed the five foreigners," Mintaka told Dayuma. "But your mother was very, very sad. They told her they had avenged your death and speared the ones who had killed and eaten you. But your mother still cried and cried. "Then Minkayi dreamed you were still alive. He said he saw you in his dream."

Maengamo took up the story. "After that your mother wanted to look for you again. Then one day the foreigners' wood-bee flew over the clearing again. Our men said they had killed its soul, but here it was buzzing again. It began to drop good gifts, and Akawo said you still lived. She went to the middle of the clearing.

"Flinging her arms heavenward like this"—by now Maengamo's arms were waving wildly as she reenacted Akawo's conversation with the wood-bee—"she cried out to it, 'Where, oh where does my daughter Dayuma live?' As your mother watched, someone on the bee pointed to the west. Your mother said you lived there."

Maengamo paused and then abruptly announced she was hungry. She blew on the dying fire and started to peel yuca to be cooked in the big black pot. As she and Mintaka busied themselves, Dayuma stared pensively at the fire now springing to life again.

Shocked and stunned by all she had learned in a few days at Limoncocha, Dayuma was facing some hard decisions.

It was just as she had thought. Her own people had killed Rachel's brother. The Aucas had not understood why the foreigners came.

"And my brother Nampa? He did not spear the foreigners?" Dayuma asked.

"No, Nampa did not spear at the Curaray, but after they were killed he went to the place where they were buried and shouted angrily, 'Why did you kill my sister Dayuma?'"

Then Maengamo reviewed the death of Dayuma's younger brother, after the spearing of the foreigners. He had been crushed by a boa while hunting in the forest. Black and blue and very ill, he lingered for a month. He had been cursed by the downriver Indians, Maengamo said, and finally died a horrible death.

Dayuma was beside herself. She had heard the details of her brother Wawae's murder. But she had expected to see Nampa again. Now he, too, was dead, she learned.

"If I had returned when I tried to run away from Ila, I would have seen Wawae again," Dayuma sobbed as she repeated the news to Rachel. "And Nampa tried to climb the vine of the wood-bee to find me. If I had returned then—"

As she finished weeping out her sadness, Dayuma said with finality, "I am never going back. My father was speared. Wawae was speared. Nampa is dead. Now I will never go back home. I won't teach you any more of my language—"

She poked a few belongings into her *shigra*, a small palm-fiber bag. Her son, Sammy, stood by, bewildered.

"Come," Dayuma said to him. "We are going."

Rachel watched as they walked down the trail and then off toward the Napo River.

For months Rachel had prayed as successive waves of sadness threatened to overcome the girl. Each blow seemed harder, and Rachel had asked for spiritual stability for Dayuma. Now the shock of hearing of her youngest brother's death, added to the details of the death of Rachel's brother at the hands of her people, was too much for the overwrought girl.

Rachel walked back to the thatched shelter, fighting tears. It was a quiet afternoon in the jungle. The clock ticked loudly. In the sultry stillness, she was praying.

"Lord, I thought that Dayuma was the one to reach her tribe, but I have always counted on You. Reach the tribe, Lord, with or without Dayuma."

# CHAPTER FIFTEEN

# "Following Him, We Will Go"

As Rachel prayed, the minutes ticked away. She was facing the future of the Auca work without Dayuma.

Suddenly the stillness was broken as shouts of commotion rose from a jungle trail where Betty Elliot had been walking with Mintaka and Maengamo. Betty came running to Rachel, calling, "What is an *imiñi?* One has bitten Maengamo, and she is in hysterics!"

Rachel could not remember what an *imiñi* was—"except that it was bad, and maybe a snake."

There seemed only one thing to do. Rachel started running down the trail through the big trees toward the river, calling to Dayuma, "A snake has bitten Maengamo! Come quickly!"

Dayuma wheeled around and shouted, "Why did you call me when I was running away?" But she quickly went back to see what had happened to Maengamo.

The *imiñi* turned out to be a scorpion, which caused Maengamo pain and discomfort but was not deadly. As Dayuma and her two aunts discussed the scorpion sting and sought remedies for it, they began to reminisce about various kinds of stings and bites in their clearing in the forest, and what was done for them.

During Maengamo's recuperation, Dayuma forgot about running away as the three Aucas talked of returning to their forest home. For weeks they had watched the kapok tree down by the lake, and already the big round pods were beginning to burst. Maengamo had told her family that if all went well and the foreigners did not kill her and Mintaka, they would return at the blooming of the kapok. The time had come for the homeward trek.

Dayuma, shaken by all the family tragedies, was not sure she wanted to go back to a home without father or brothers to welcome her. She wept for them occasionally. But one day she came to Rachel with a smile and tearless eyes.

"Now I have finished crying for my brothers." She began to talk about the trip into the forest with her aunts.

"If you don't return with us, my brother will be furious," Mintaka had told Dayuma. Gikita had wanted Mintaka to go with the five foreigners on the Curaray and bring back a report from the outside world. Now, after years of searching for Dayuma, they would face certain death merely to report having seen her. They could not return to her family without her.

But Dayuma continued to wonder about many things. After an absence of nearly twelve years, would her own people accept her, or regard her as a foreigner? What would they think of her clothes? Should she go all the way to her family clearing? Would they let her return again to the outside world?

Now, when Dayuma needed encouragement, Rachel shared the lesson of Christ as Shepherd of His sheep. But the lesson's truth was purely theoretical for Indians who had never known sheep and their habits. As a timely providence, a mountain sheep was taken to Limoncocha by the United States Air Mission as a decoy for jaguar hunting and left in Dayuma's care. Rachel used it to illustrate otherwise obscure verses of Scripture. The sheep became attached to Dayuma and learned to recognize and follow her voice. It would not go ahead of her on the jungle trails, nor would it drink from the swift streams. One night it fell into a pit from which it could not extricate itself. When Dayuma passed near, it heard her voice and bleated. She climbed down into the pit and rescued it.

"When he has brought out all his own, he goes on ahead of them, and his sheep follow him because they know his voice."

(John 10:4 NIV) was a Bible truth illustrated by the unusual provision of the sheep at the base. "Following Him, we will go" became the Auca version of obeying the Good Shepherd.

As the time drew near for the three Aucas to leave Limoncocha for the Curaray trail, Rachel reminded Dayuma that she would soon be on her own with the Good Shepherd; she would need to recognize His voice and follow Him. She reviewed the Bible lesson in preparation for the first missionary journey into the Auca tribe.

Eventually the little party set off on the trail leading away from Arajuno, heavy-laden with food for the trip, gifts for their families, and three "foreigners' pups."

As the three Auca women disappeared on the jungle trail, a missionary standing close by remarked, "I wonder if we'll ever see them again?" Rachel recalls that as she said good-bye to Dayuma, she was confident of seeing her again, but that she didn't know whether it would be in two weeks or two years.

Rachel wrote to her praying friends on September 2, the day the trio departed:

"Dayuma has a deep desire to teach her people God's Word, to see her family again, and to try to bring harmony within the tribe and with the outside world. On the other hand, she knows full well the darkness she is entering.

"By the time this letter reaches you, with God's blessing, all three may be back once again in what is left of the village where Nate started making gift-drops. Need I tell you that my heart has gone with her, and that I encouraged her to stay and teach her people without hurrying back if all goes well? Need I remind you that she is still a babe in Christ, and that the whole responsibility of introducing her people to the Lord Jesus rests with her? Pray for us as we continue our part in language study that will lead to a translation of His Word. Need I describe the darkness of heart and mind of a people who fear only what will happen to a dead body, but have no thought of what will happen to a living soul? Need I ask you to stand with Dayuma and me in prevailing prayer?

"Before they left, both Mintaka and Maengamo had begun to pray to the God in heaven as Dayuma taught them. Shall we not take this as a cloud the size of a man's hand and trust for the showers to come?...

"I am now so thankful He led me to give top priority to teaching Dayuma, for 'faith cometh by hearing, and hearing by the Word of God....' "

A week later Rachel wrote to friends, "I have had no word since they left, but it is the prayer of my heart that the Lord will demonstrate the power of His Word through this tribe which has been so publicized. The savagery has not been exaggerated—if anything, it has not yet been told....

"All that I have been able to teach Dayuma of His Word she has committed to memory. Will you pray that the Lord Himself will protect the truths of it. I have been grateful to hear her tell Bible stories with great accuracy as I have listened to her teaching Mintaka and Maengamo. Will you pray that she will be Spirit-led and kept free from the seething hatreds of the tribe?"

Rachel also wrote her parents that there was no word from the Aucas. "No news may well be good news—and we walk by faith, not by sight."

A letter written by Dr. Edman from Wheaton College on September 12, 1958, breathed a contagious spirit of faith and hope:

"On every hand there is much intercession for Dayuma as she returns to her people. The principalities and powers of darkness will know in advance that the Holy Spirit is coming near, and there can be the same kind of opposition to her as the disciples experienced in the storm while crossing over to the shore of the Gadarenes. However, the Master of tempest brought them safely through; and on the morrow the demonized man was fully delivered. We trust for those who long have been in bondage to the evil one.

"How wonderful to know that our Lord's eyes 'run to and fro throughout the whole earth, to show himself strong in the behalf of them whose heart is perfect toward him.' He can give Dayuma understanding far beyond all the gracious and helpful instruction she has received, so as to make plain and pertinent the way of salvation. We trust there will be the same response as given by Chief Tariri years ago in Peru."

During Dayuma's absence, Rachel took Sammy along to the Cofan jungle tribe to visit Mr. and Mrs. Bub Borman, Wycliffe

translators. Rachel stayed with Mrs. Borman and her small son at
the isolated station while her husband and another translator made
a survey trip on jungle rivers in search of other tribes needing Bible
translation.

The Cofanes lived in the opposite direction from the Aucas, and
their customs were different. They wore the long, loose-flowing
cushma common to several jungle tribes of Ecuador and Peru.
Instead of round balsa earplugs, characteristic of the Aucas, the
Cofan men plucked brilliant marigolds for their smaller ear holes,
or put a feather ornament through the hole in their nose.

While in the Cofan tribe, Rachel stood by on the radio set twice
a day for news that Dayuma might have come back out of the forest. But the weeks wore on with no word. Anxiety mounted. Rumors
were abroad that Dayuma had been killed, inasmuch as she was not
spotted from the air. Rachel heard nothing of these rumors until
she received cards of condolence from friends in the United States.

Then after almost a month, the joyous radio message reached
Rachel. Dayuma and several companions were in Arajuno. The
same morning a Wycliffe plane was on its way from Limoncocha to
pick up Rachel and Sammy and take them to Dayuma.

On October 3, Rachel wrote her parents, "You have probably
heard by now that Dayuma, along with Mintaka and Maengamo,
plus one of Naenkiwi's wives and baby, and three girls and two boys
arrived in Arajuno last Thursday. Marj happened to be here, and
she and Betty met them as they came in. Dayuma was in the lead
singing, 'Jesus loves me, this I know'—*in English!* By the time I got
here, she was pretty keyed up, and it has taken me a while to get the
picture in focus. She brought an invitation for Betty and me to
return with them, and has given orders about building a house for
us.

"I had not heard anything definite about her for twenty-seven
days, and had promised to fly over at the full moon if we could
arrange it. My confident trust was put in the Lord. By full moon, I
was reunited with Dayuma. She just told me tonight about her
trip...."

ᔆ ᔆ ᔆ ᔆ

Dayuma, grown unaccustomed to forest trails, had become very weary and footsore as she traveled back to her old home. Her feet became swollen and thorn-pricked.

The three women took the old Shell Oil trail, thus bypassing the Quichua Indian village, and built their own shelter the first night. The second day they traveled through the forest on the Auca side of the Curaray, cutting a trail as they went. But after hours of toil, they found themselves at their starting point. They had lost their way and were chopping a wide circular trail.

At sunset they stopped by a small jungle stream. "Here there used to be lots and lots of fish," Dayuma remembered, so Mintaka and Maengamo took their nets and went fishing. Dayuma was delegated to build the shelter. Quickly, she cut off the leaves of the low *yarina* palm and hastily constructed a tiny shelter. She also built a ground fire. Exhausted, she could do no more. By the time Mintaka and Maengamo returned with a mess of fish, thunder was roaring and lightning was flashing, and they were suddenly aware of a huge storm front of dark clouds moving downriver toward them. Maengamo took one look at the lightly-constructed shelter and offered to chop down a *tipa* palm for protection from the storm that was certain to come. By now it was late and getting dark, and Dayuma protested.

"Let's just ask the Lord to keep it from raining on us," she said. Maengamo and Mintaka assented, Dayuma prayed, and all three watched as the big black clouds retreated upriver.

The next day they continued through the trailless jungle. On one of the beaches they saw a huge jaguar lying in the sun, but it woke up and disappeared into the cane patch before they had time to be concerned. By evening, Dayuma felt she could go no farther.

Tired and hungry, she began to talk to the Lord as Rachel had taught her.

"Shall we stay here?" Dayuma asked Him.

"Yes," came the answer.

As Dayuma took her bearings and talked with her aunts, she realized this was the spot on the Tiwaeno River where she had lived as a young girl. The jungle had reclaimed the clearing when the family migrated.

"What shall we eat?" was the next question Dayuma put to the Lord. The yuca drink they had brought with them was long since exhausted. As if in answer to her plea, Maengamo remembered that years before when they lived on the Tiwaeno they had had a sweet potato patch growing on one of the beaches. They hurried upriver and found enough sweet potatoes to make a refreshing and satisfying drink.

The women cleared weeds and chopped jungle growth. They killed a big snake, and also saw the footprints of an oversized jaguar. They wondered whether they should stay temporarily on the Tiwaeno, or press on toward the family clearing. As darkness fell and they prayed and talked together, Maengamo decided she would leave at dawn and go to tell Akawo and the family that Dayuma was back in the forest. Mintaka would wait with Dayuma.

In the morning, after Maengamo's departure, Dayuma prayed. She asked the Lord, "What shall we eat?"

"Fish," came the answer.

So Dayuma and Mintaka made spears from cane that grew by the river and went spearfishing, using the old jungle method. In a short time, Dayuma had speared ten big fish.

By sunset of the second day, when Maengamo had not returned, Mintaka became apprehensive and said, "Let's flee back to the foreigners." Dayuma objected. If Maengamo did not return, they must follow her footsteps in the morning to see what had happened to her.

It was now almost dark, and keen disappointment overwhelmed Dayuma. For hours she had been looking downriver, listening for the tread of bare feet on the forest trail.

Had her mother died while Maengamo and Mintaka were on the outside? Or did Akawo not want to see her daughter after all? Perhaps by this time she was resigned that Dayuma and her aunts had been killed and had consequently moved back downriver, deep into the jungle.

She thought of the bright, shiny pair of foreigners' scissors she had brought for her mother to replace the sharp shells which Aucas used for cutting—and the big ax head. She was almost sorry now that she had carried it over the trail—it was so heavy. Perhaps her mother would never use it.

As the last patches of daylight fell on the trail by the rushing stream, Dayuma picked up the three pups she had carried in from the outside as a gift for her mother. She was sure her mother would be pleased. The Aucas had never had any dogs! She then walked down the beach for a last look around the bend before dark.

Suddenly the pups began to bark in quick, shrill yips, straining to give a grown-up warning of an approaching noise. Dayuma stood completely still as she listened. She heard voices, and then the thump, thump, thump of feet on the nearby beach. Was it Maengamo? And who was with her—Akawo? In the dim light, Dayuma saw a bronze body round the bend. Could it be...?

"Dayuma!"

She leaped with joy at the familiar voice of her mother.

"I thought my daughter had died long, long ago—and now I see you alive!" Akawo's voice broke.

Dayuma swallowed hard. "I thought you had died long ago, Mother!" she blurted out. For a moment she was awkwardly conscious of her clothes. And now she was much taller than her mother.

"I brought these foreigners' pups for you, Mother," she continued in a steadier voice.

Akawo chuckled with delight and reached out to take the little dogs that were still yapping importantly. She lavished on them all the affection she felt for Dayuma.

It was quite dark when Kimo and his wife, Dawa, arrived. Maengamo and Minkayi found their way to the fire soon afterward. Everyone was laughing and talking excitedly as Mintaka flopped the smoked fish on the banana leaves spread on the ground by the fire. A hungry, happy family fell to devouring the delicious meal.

"The others will come tomorrow," Akawo said.

"Will my sister Gimari come?" Dayuma asked.

"Yes, she will come with your Uncle Gikita."

Dayuma was relieved. Maengamo had told her at Limoncocha that Gimari's husband, the terrible Naenkiwi, was brutally speared and buried alive. Akawo had been willing for Gimari to return to the family circle, but her sister Oba refused to have her. Oba had married Dyuwi, whom Akawo had originally selected as Gimari's husband before she ran away with Naenkiwi. Thus, Oba feared the wiles of her sister. Gimari had gone to live with her mother-in-law, Dyiko, who was related by marriage to Uncle Gikita. Dayuma was happy that Gimari would be coming with Gikita, for she was eager to see her.

"Gikita didn't want to come," laughed Maengamo, "but I told him that the foreigners would kill him if he didn't—so he will be here tomorrow."

Everyone laughed except Dayuma. Why didn't her Uncle Gikita want to come to see her? Did he think she had become a foreigner?

The next day others of Dayuma's family group continued to arrive on the Tiwaeno. Maengamo had sent word to all the Aucas surrounding the big clearing that Dayuma was back. Within a few days more than fifty grown-ups and children of the family group had hurried over the trail to see her. With Uncle Gikita and his family came Gimari, carrying baby Bai in a bark sling. When the little boy saw Dayuma, he began to scream. He was frightened by her clothes. Her hairstyle marked her as a stranger, too. Oba and Dyuwi came with their baby girl, Adyibae, who also cried in terror at the sight of Dayuma. This greeting was most humiliating for a fond aunt eager to see her nephew and niece. Dayuma's little sister Ana, born after she had fled the forest, was very shy at first. Very quickly, however, she accepted Dayuma into the family circle. Before many days had passed, Dayuma was exercising the privileges of a big sister by spanking Ana with nettles for being lazy.

Akawo took over the family cooking in her big clay pot, as she had many years ago, only now it was little Ana who brought the water from the jungle stream instead of Dayuma.

Dayuma ate her fill of the delicious jungle food for the first time in many years. Minkayi had brought her "lots of monkeys," and her mother provided the big mess of fish promised upon Dayuma's return.

Tiny palm-thatched huts were hastily constructed close to one another as the Aucas cut back the jungle growth and hung hammocks around the log fires they had built on the ground. Foreigners were a favorite topic of conversation as they retired in their hammocks at night. Dayuma's family had dozens of questions about them.

"We were afraid. We thought the foreigners would kill us and eat us," said some of the Aucas, who inquired what they were really like.

"And that is just what the foreigners think about you!" laughed Dayuma.

Gradually, the family group began to talk about the five foreigners they had speared on the Curaray.

"I was very sad when those foreigners were killed," said Dabu, who had not been present when the men of the clearing went to spear. "I cried when I heard about it. Later I went to the beach and cut down the big tree in which they had built their house. I felled it across the beach so that no more foreigners would come in and be killed."

As Dayuma told her people the other side of the story, they said sadly, "Not understanding, we did not do well."

They still had questions about foreigners, however. A short time before Dayuma's return, a foreign explorer had come into their territory.

"Whenever we came near, he tried to shoot us," they said. "After five days he became afraid. He killed himself with his own gun. Then we speared his body and burned the house he had occupied. His body rotted, but the buzzards did not eat him. He was surely a devil."

Dayuma's people wondered which foreigners they could trust, and she assured them that "the ones who bring you gifts in the plane are good foreigners." She told of many good outsiders she had known and with whom she had lived, and of their land far away where she had visited. For hours each night as they lay in their hammocks, warming their bare feet over the dying embers, Dayuma entertained them with stories of the many giant wood-bees in which she had flown. Her hands were constantly in motion as she described her long trip from Hacienda Ila to Quito in the captain's little wood-bee, then the long, long flight over the big water in a huge one. She even told her people how the skeleton and skin of the wood-bees were created. She spoke of her trip to New York where she saw a mammoth canoe carrying many wood-bees on its back. All in all, her knowledge of the flying creatures impressed those who had seen them only high overhead.

Her family wanted to know what foreigners ate and what kind of houses they lived in. Dayuma confessed she had often missed the meat of the forest, for foreigners did not have much meat.

They ate many other things, but even if she ate a lot, she was still hungry for meat. She told them of the big houses where many foreigners lived together. Instead of walking on trails, they sat down in "wood-bees that go on the ground" and went very fast. There were so many of these in big trails in the foreigners' land that one had to watch or he would be killed by them.

Many of the foreigners that Dayuma had known "carved" on paper most of the time. "Why did they do that?" the Aucas wanted to know. Dayuma explained that they were carving God's words for other people, like the Aucas, who had never heard about the true God. She then told them of what she had learned from God's carving. But her stories about heaven were more fantastic than those of the United States. Her mother and sisters laughed and said, "Why do you talk like that, Dayuma?" Everyone laughed derisively— except two. Old Mima listened carefully and asked questions about God. Young Dawa, who had been captured from downriver after Dayuma left the forest, was eager to know more. She had become Kimo's wife and was now a part of Dayuma's family group.

As Dayuma told her people what she had seen and learned in almost a dozen years in the outside world, they in turn told her all that had transpired since that fateful day when Moipa speared her father, Tyaento.

Dayuma watched Gimari care for her baby, Bai. She thought of Naenkiwi, Gimari's husband. When he had finally met his end, little Bai would have been thrown into his father's grave alive had Gimari not grabbed him and fled. And there was old Dyiko, Gimari's mother-in-law, who had come with her daughter Nombo and her children to see Dayuma. Nombo's husband, Gaba, had been speared by mistake by Naenkiwi a short time before his own death. Indeed, many sad things had happened.

As the fires on the Tiwaeno burned low in the deep night and the Aucas slumbered in their hammocks, Dayuma lay awake and gazed at the same bright stars she had watched as a little girl. The rushing water sang nearby, accompanied by the loud chirping of crickets and the call of the forest night birds. The howling and chattering of many kinds of monkeys swelled the jungle jargon—sweet music to one long nostalgic for the sounds of home. As she listened, Dayuma reviewed what she had been hearing each day from the lips of old Uncle Gikita, and her mother, Akawo, and all her relatives who had suffered and survived the many spearings since she had left the forest of death. It all had a familiar ring.

The next morning, as Dayuma watched little Bai and Tamaenta toddle by the edge of the Tiwaeno River, she was glad they had been spared. She knew, however, that unless they were taught about the Lord of love, they too would grow up to spear and be speared, to avenge and be avenged.

Around the fires on the Tiwaeno, Dayuma heard more unpleasant news. Gikita and the other men had readied the spears for another trip downriver. It was time to settle accounts with those who had killed Wawae and Wamoñi.

She pleaded with Uncle Gikita not to go and prayed to God he would take her suggestion. Wawae and Wamoñi were dead. What good would it do now to kill those who had speared them so many years ago? The God she had come to tell them about wanted them to forgive their enemies and not spear in exchange.

Kimo quickly agreed. He was tired of spearings.

And as Dayuma's family settled in and built more shelters on the banks of the Tiwaeno, Uncle Gikita talked less and less of his trip downriver, and the spears were set aside.

# CHAPTER SIXTEEN

# Home on the Tiwaeno

Within a few weeks, Dayuma's people on the banks of the Tiwaeno had reviewed for her a twelve-year history of the Aucas, upriver and down. There had been a steady succession of spearings since she left—an uninterrupted march of unnatural, premature death. None of Dayuma's grandparents was living now, even though her mother, Akawo, was not very old. Her Uncle Gikita, much younger than her mother, was the oldest man of the vanishing group.

But for Dayuma, the picture was different because *she* had changed. She was not the same Dayuma who had left the forest with hate and revenge. From the day Rachel had first communicated in faltering Auca the words of God's carving, life had taken on new meaning. For over a year, Dayuma had been with foreigners like Rachel who "lived well" because they obeyed God. She had visited in their land far away where people did not spear one another. Could this ever come to pass here in her forest where people *lived*, apparently, to spear one another? Only God's carving could make a difference. It was God who had uprooted hate and planted love in her heart. She had found herself praying even for Moipa's surviving relatives, that they would hear of the true God. Months before in Sulphur Springs, she had also begun to pray for those once-hated enemies: the downriver Indians.

A plane flying low over the Tiwaeno reminded Dayuma that Rachel and Betty would be wondering what had happened to her. She was hidden by the big trees, and the plane had not seen her. They might think that her people had killed her. It was almost one full moon since she had said good-bye to them at Arajuno.

When Dayuma came into the forest with her aunts, the germs of foreigners' colds had traveled with them. With no natural resistance, a number of the Aucas had fallen sick with heavy colds. Mima and Akawo were among those most gravely affected. Dayuma was concerned about her mother's condition. But she thought too of Rachel and Betty waiting on the outside for news from the forest, and she decided it was necessary to bring them word.

As she talked with her aunts Mintaka and Maengamo about the return trip to the outside, Dayuma also talked to God about one matter very important to her. Upon her arrival in the tribe, she had found Maruja, the Quichua girl captured by the Aucas when they speared her husband the year before at the time her aunts went to the outside. Maruja was living in Uncle Gikita's home. It was too late to help Maruja's husband, but Dayuma was eager to return the captured girl to her mother, Jacinta, who had been so kind in nursing Dayuma back to health.

Would Uncle Gikita release Maruja? Dayuma was troubled. One day she decided to make her request. Uncle Gikita thought a few moments, and Dayuma tried to read his face. To her intense relief, he said yes, Maruja could go back to her family.

Dayuma was also grateful for the word from her people that Rachel and Betty would be welcome to hang their hammocks in shelters being built for them overlooking the Tiwaeno.

Nights of long discussions around the flickering fire preceded the return trip to the foreigners' world. Who would go with Dayuma? It was plain that none of the men was interested. In spite of the good reports about outsiders, they were unprepared to go. Kimo remembered the Quichuas' guns when he and Dawa had

gone to the Oglán village with Mintaka and Maengamo the year
before. However, the two venturesome aunts, undaunted, were
ready for another trip. Mintaka's young son Gingata would go with
his mother. Wato, now almost grown to maturity, was eager for the
trip, as well as her companion, Ñaeno, of nearly equal age. Ipa,
Naenkiwi's young widow, would go carrying her baby Tamaenta.
Ipa's young brother Kinta joined the party. Gimari said that baby
Bai was too big and fat to carry that distance over the trail. She
would wait on the Tiwaeno for Dayuma to return with the foreign
women. Mima's daughter Gakamo, the youngest girl of the travelers,
would go along in spite of her mother's illness.

Dayuma was happy that Uncle Gikita did not change his mind
about Maruja. As the Quichua girl left Tiwaeno with the group of
Aucas, she wore clothes that Dayuma had given her. Mintaka and
Maengamo also started out with the clothing they had brought
from the outside world. It never occurred to the others that clothes
were worn on such occasions.

The women and children, chattering and chuckling with excitement, were soon out of sight of the clearing and splashed with glee
as they crossed the small stream. They were in high spirits as they
bounded lithely over the wooded trails toward Tapir River. Then
another hilarious dip in the refreshing water—and with a yodel
known only to Aucas, they were off through the forest toward Grape
Tree River. Dayuma and her aunts were happy leaders on the familiar trail as they climbed up hills and down jungle valleys, clambering
surefootedly over fallen logs and through thorny tangles, slashing
with their machetes when the trail was otherwise impassable.

After sleeping one night in the jungle, the Indian travelers
arrived at the Quichua village on the Oglán River. There was animated discussion in the Quichua huts that night when Maruja
rejoined her amazed family.

The party next followed the old Shell Oil trail, and finally
emerged at Arajuno on September 25. With her usual exuberance,
Dayuma was singing happily when Betty Elliot and Marj Saint spotted her leading the group down the airstrip toward the mission
houses.

It seemed a long time to Dayuma before Rachel and Sammy flew in from the Cofan tribe with Captain Griffin in the Helioplane. The young Aucas of the party were impressed with the foreigners' wood-bee about which they had heard so much. Veteran air-traveler Dayuma proudly showed them the inside and explained its operation.

✍ ✍ ✍ ✍

There was hardly time in Arajuno for Dayuma to tell Rachel all she had learned during the month with her people. Dayuma did bring some very important news though. Two of the group who had come to welcome her on the Tiwaeno had not laughed when she told them about God's carving. All the others—including her mother and sisters—had laughed and said, "Why do you talk like that, Dayuma?" But two, old Mima and young Dawa, both women from downriver, had listened well. The night before Dayuma left, Dawa had said, "Now you are going. Tell me again about God's Son so that I won't forget while you are gone." Dayuma did so, and urged her to teach others while she was away. Old Mima had listened again and had asked questions about Jesus.

Dayuma thanked the Lord over and over again as she and Rachel prayed together that her people let her come back out, and that they invited Rachel and Betty to go in with her.

In Arajuno Dayuma told Rachel of Akawo's illness and of her desire to return quickly. "Don't let my mother die before we go back into the forest," she prayed.

The group prepared for the trip to the Tiwaeno. The Auca members of the party needed little time for planning a return. The foreigners' things—clothes and cooking utensils—given them at Arajuno were ready for transport. But for several days Rachel and Betty pondered and pared their provisions down to a minimum load to be carried over jungle trails. It was a historic expedition that set out from Arajuno on October 6. For three of the members— Rachel, Betty, and Betty's four-year-old daughter, Valerie—it would be an unprecedented experience. The Aucas were now wearing clothes, the gifts of Dr. and Mrs. Tidmarsh. Missionaries in charge of the Arajuno station, the Tidmarshes had participated in the gift-drops for many months after the five men were killed at Palm

Beach. The Indian women and girls proudly carried shiny new foreigners' pots. One of the Quichuas bore the special burden of little
Valerie Elliot.

The cargo included equipment for two-way radio contact—a
lifeline to the outside world. However, Rachel and Betty relied more
heavily on the volume of prayer ascending around the world for the
safety and success of the venture. Concerned friends filled the air
with prayers and kept their radios tuned or watched the incoming
mail for news of the unique missionary journey.

The travelers said farewell to a small group of missionaries and
Quichua Christians as they walked to the end of the airstrip. There
Dayuma gathered her party together and prayed in Auca, asking
God to go with them on the trip and protect them from snakebites
and jaguars on the trail. She prayed earnestly that her people back
in the forest would receive the two white women well. Then they
disappeared on the trail that soon merged into the tall grasslands
beyond.

For several hours they followed the fairly level, narrow, but
solid road that had been paved with stones by the Shell Company
for its trucks. It was the trail originally traveled by gold prospectors
and rubber men, but had long since fallen into disuse as enterprises
one by one had been forced to retreat from Auca territory. A good
distance down the trail, they found an abandoned dump truck
which for years had been rusting in isolation. Dayuma explained
the phenomenon to Indians who had never seen a "wood-bee that
goes on the ground."

After hiking through open forest that showed signs of former
clearings, the travelers came to the Dayono River, halfway between
Arajuno and the Oglán. From here, the Dayono flowed deep into
Auca country. Without changing pace, the Aucas crossed the river
in water well above their knees, followed by the Quichua carriers
and the foreigners. As they crossed, the Aucas reviewed an attack
upon explorers who used this water gateway to venture into the forbidden land. Traversing the familiar river also reminded them of
their family history, and they lost themselves in stories. The river
itself had been named for Dyuwi's grandmother Dayo, who fished
downriver with *barbasco* poison. One day while fishing, she had

been bitten by a snake. She was pregnant at the time and had returned home in great pain. Born prematurely, the child died, and soon after, the mother died, too.

As they left the more level land surrounding Arajuno, they ducked under branches of big trees and climbed over fallen logs across the trail. At times they crossed shallow swamps on felled trees to keep from sinking into the deep mud. There were scenic views down deep valleys where racing streams below tossed up billows of white foam. Occasionally they heard bird songs—the celestial, flutelike call of the *wiiwa* bird, or the squawk of a flamboyant macaw as it screeched overhead. They crossed deep ravines with tall jungle trees rising majestically. At the halfway mark the group reached the winding course of the Oglán. They picked their way through the huge rocks of the riverbed and continued on the trail now leading through steep, forested hills.

In spite of the exotic beauty of the trail, Rachel began to tire. "Just two more big hills and one little one," Dayuma encouraged. "It won't be long now."

By late afternoon the weary travelers finally spotted the planted fields of the Quichuas, high above the village on the banks of the Curaray.

After a welcome night's sleep on the ground of an Indian hut and with a replenished supply of yuca and bananas, some of the Tiwaeno-bound party set out down the Curaray in two small dugout canoes. The others took to the trail that followed the river or crossed it at other points. Dayuma accompanied Rachel and Betty and Valerie in the heavy-laden dugout canoes. She was tense with her new responsibility, but happy that this day had finally come. The polers skillfully guided the canoes over occasional rapids and were soon rhythmically shifting their weight from the back to the forward foot. On one side of the river, a sheer rock wall dropped down to the water. Overhanging trees or logs that had been carried downstream by the strong current had to be carefully avoided, particularly by the poler in forward position, whose job it was to steer the course. At times the passengers were soaked to the skin as they rode through the splashing rapids of the Curaray. The party traveled downriver to the mouth of the Oglán, marked by several large sandbars and wide, sandy beaches. Dayuma pointed pensively to a small shaded spot on the bank where her husband and baby boy were buried. She reminded Rachel that she had also battled with death at that time.

Trained Indian eyes were ever alert for birds or animals that might appear at the edge of the forest bordering the beaches. Occasionally a wild turkey or other game would be sighted and shot with the guns the Quichuas had brought along.

The Aucas who had gone on foot were often visible through the trees, and could be seen wading along the beaches or swimming to the opposite shore. The clothes with which they proudly started out from Arajuno had long since been set aside as the Indians once again enjoyed the freedom of the open forest. At mid-morning everyone stopped on a beach for nourishment. Balls of yuca dough were unwrapped from banana leaves, mixed with river water in gourd bowls, and consumed by the thirsty group.

The travelers were aware that they were penetrating deeper into Auca territory. "Let your long hair down," Dayuma advised Rachel. "Then if the other Aucas attack, they will know you are a woman. Our people always spear the men first." The Quichuas frequently checked the guns lying in ready position near each poler.

They soon continued down the spacious, spreading Curaray toward the mouth of Grape Tree River. Along the beaches were occasional abandoned shelters built by Quichua fishermen. Rustic platforms for smoking fish were falling unused into the sand. For months now the river had been practically deserted for fear of the Aucas. By four o'clock in the afternoon, the canoes were anchored to the navigators' poles, which were firmly planted in the solid sandy bank by the river. Experienced Indians immediately began constructing lean-to shelters on the beach, using stalks of wild cane to support roofs made of the long, arching leaves. A few well-aimed strokes of machetes, and the encampment was ready. Driftwood bleached in the jungle sun made a roaring fire. By dark the canny hunters were back with birds and small game to be roasted and eaten before the campers retired in the shelters surrounding the glowing coals. Quichuas and Aucas, who in years past had attacked and counterattacked, communicated with smiles and gestures and shared their meat as they ate on the sandy beach.

Early the next morning the dugouts headed up Grape Tree River, a smaller stream pushing its way through dense jungle. Poling was slower as they bucked the current in the narrow channels, and occasionally it was necessary to chop a path through trees that had fallen over the stream. Often the party would get out and walk the beaches while the polers pulled the heavy-laden canoes over the shallow rapids. Branches of fragrant flowering trees arched gracefully across the rushing stream. Beautifully colored jungle birds would dart in front of the canoe or dip across the water.

The Aucas were irresistibly drawn to quiet waters at the bends of the river where fish abounded. The young boys were now carrying long, thin chonta spears as they waded into the deeper waters, eyes alert for fish, and encouraged by the others. Ipa and Maengamo stood by and called to Kinta as they sighted the fish, and Mintaka was spurring her young son Gingata to action. The younger girls flanked the fishermen to catch the fish as they were tossed over. Dayuma suppressed her desire to fish and stayed in the canoe with the foreigners.

The journey upriver was a memorable one for Rachel as Dayuma reminded her of tribal incidents recalled by the familiar jungle landmarks. With every stroke of the polers, Rachel was aware that she was coming close to the fulfillment of a hope that had been deferred for many years.

"There is the beach where Moipa attacked the gold hunters," Dayuma said. The men had crossed over to the Tiwaeno, stolen the Aucas' yuca and cooking bananas, and returned to camp on the Grape Tree River. But they were volleyed with spears in the night and had abandoned the camp in the darkness. The next morning Moipa and his men had helped themselves to the foreigners' possessions. This was the world once ruled by Moipa's spears.

At the mouth of the Tapir River, the Quichua polers hesitated, looked to Dayuma for direction, then guided their dugouts up the smaller river. By the unwritten law known only to forest men, they were well aware that this was the river marking the point beyond which foreigners never dared to go.

The Tapir River was fringed with exquisite palms of many varieties and stately bamboo bending with the breeze. The swift water that became shallower as they approached the end of their canoe trip forced them to stop and laboriously chop a passage through a huge fallen log. After tying the dugout canoes high on the beach with strong jungle vines, the Quichuas adjusted their packs once more and followed the Aucas and the foreigners on the tiny stream leading off to the forest trail.

Maengamo took the lead in search for the almost-invisible trail and cut the overhanging branches as she went. This was virgin forest, and the animal trails to the water holes were more clearly marked than those of man. The others followed her slowly up the steep hills and across the narrow ridge.

Dayuma pointed out a cross path known to the Aucas as Moipa's trail. They were on the homestretch.

"We are almost there," said Dayuma as she heard the stream playing over the rocks around the bend. She was unable to suppress her excitement. She chuckled contentedly while she pointed out the old sweet-potato patch that her father had planted years ago, and the site of the old yuca field. The trail entered the Tiwaeno and followed the crystal-clear stream.

"That is where Gimari was born," she said as they left the river and climbed the bank.

She led the way over the trail on the bank of the stream. Trees overhung the path to the clearing, and a wild cane patch shielded the huts from view. Then the trail entered the Tiwaeno again, following the stream.

The sweetest of pictures greeted Rachel as she rounded the bend. There in the gleaming sun were the little thatched huts of the Aucas, nestled in the small clearing cut out of the high forest.

Kimo rose serenely to welcome the party and stood watching, arms folded, as they filed up the trail. He seemed like a handsome statue as the afternoon sun played on his well-developed muscles. A pleased expression betrayed his curiosity. His young wife, Dawa, smiled a welcome as the foreign women approached her. Gimari, holding her baby, laughed shyly and spoke to Dayuma as the travelers gathered in the clearing.

Kimo, his wife, Dawa, and Dayuma's sister Gimari were the only ones on the Tiwaeno clearing when Dayuma returned with the foreign women. Kimo proudly showed them the big shelter he was constructing for them.

"All alone I built it," he said with a boyish smile. It had been slow work to fell trees and haul them in alone. The shelter was not finished, but Kimo had fulfilled Dayuma's parting instructions.

"Where are the others?" asked Dayuma.

Kimo said they had returned downriver for a new supply of food, but that he had stayed behind to wait for the foreigners he hoped would come.

He did not add the fact that the other relatives had left in fear. As they faced the possibility of outsiders entering their land, they had become apprehensive and returned to their former clearing.

CHAPTER SEVENTEEN

# "What Is His Name?"

In the afternoon of October 8, Rachel penned her first letter to her parents from the Tiwaeno clearing. It was taken out by the returning Quichua carriers. "The welcome could not have been more friendly," she wrote. "You'd think these bronze girls were debutantes entertaining, and that this happened every day. They are really charmers. Kimo's wife has no children yet. Gimari has a darling fat baby, Bai, who is another of Naenkiwi's children.

"The little huts are so low I can hardly get into them.... It seems the most natural thing in the world to me to be here, a thing I felt the Lord was leading me to over five years ago. Do pray that this situation will be workable and will accomplish the Lord's purposes....

"Kimo's wife, Dawa, is from the downriver group. Although the natural situation would never take her back to them, I pray that she may be one of the contacts that will lead them to Him, too. It is a larger group than this one, and they speak the same language."

Rachel watched from the cluster of thatched huts as the young boys hurried off to spearfish upriver, trailing their long fishing spears behind them. Maengamo hung her hammock and was off across the river to bring back yuca for her family. The younger girls went to the stream with their clay pots for water. Ipa, shadowed by her tiny son Tamaenta, went to the forest to bring firewood.

Young Gakamo did not seem to know what to do with herself. As soon as she had arrived on the clearing, Dawa had informed her of her mother Mima's death caused by the foreigners' colds. She had been buried downriver. Dayuma, too, felt the loss, since Mima had listened eagerly to the stories of God's Son.

Betty and her little daughter moved their few possessions into the empty shelter adjoining Maengamo's hut. Dayuma decided to sleep with the young girls in their hut nearby, and Maengamo offered Rachel three long pieces of bamboo to make a bed on the ground beneath her palm-thatched roof. There was no privacy until the curtains of night were automatically drawn. The jungle moon was clearly visible, enhanced by its reflection in the swift waters of the Tiwaeno, which played melodiously on the rocks. It was a sociable life, and the Aucas were a gregarious people. Huts were close enough to permit hammock-to-hammock conversation.

At dawn the day after the arrival of Dayuma and her friends, Kimo took the forest trail to the old family clearing. He had seen the foreign women for himself and wanted to persuade the others to return to the Tiwaeno.

Rachel and Betty spent the day becoming acquainted with their Indian family. "Dawa is a real charmer," Rachel noted in her diary. "She looks like an Oriental princess—graceful, smiling, and well-poised. Gimari looks older than her Palm Beach pictures, but she still has those beautiful long, dark lashes framing shiny black eyes. As I sat on the log beside the girls, you would have thought this happened every day…. They would be perfectly at home in the White House, I'm sure, and just as socially acceptable with a bit of clothing on."

Dayuma had warned Rachel that the speech of her people in the forest would be fast and difficult for a foreigner to follow. Communication on a simple conversational level was possible, however.

"Dayuma lived at my house," Rachel said to Gimari as they sat sunning themselves on the balsa log. "She is like my little sister. Now we are happy to be here."

Gimari was a pitiful figure on the buoyant Tiwaeno scene. No longer was she the winsome maiden who had gone to the Curaray to see the foreigners. Disillusioned and listless, she lived alone with Bai in a tiny, dark hut she had thatched down to the ground and which sufficed for her hammock and fire. Only necessities for herself or her son drew her out of gloomy seclusion. Rachel watched for opportunities to chat with Gimari.

"Kimo left this morning to go downriver," she told Rachel in a conversation inside her hut.

"Where is your mother, Akawo?"

"She is downriver. Perhaps she will come...."

Ordinarily, one day was required to travel over the trail to the family clearing downstream. However, at sunset of the day Kimo left, there was a shout on the Tiwaeno, "They are coming!" With Dayuma in the lead, everyone ran to the riverbank. Among the Auca girls there had been speculative questions: Would Akawo come? Would she be wearing the dress that Dayuma had given her when she first came in from the outside? She will put it on when she reaches the river, just before coming here, they concluded. Their prediction was right. Dayuma's mother, Akawo, was the first to arrive—and there were unmistakable signs that the wrinkled dress, wadded in a ball as the old mother fairly flew over the trail to Dayuma, had just been put on. And she was carrying the three pups.

"Dear old Akawo was trembling from sheer joy and excitement," Rachel noted. "Her wrinkled face has a permanent smile—and she talks constantly, as though we understand every word. How I wish that my mother could have seen her joy! She was older than I had expected her to be—but evidently a character and a personality in her own right."

Akawo's delight at Dayuma's return with the foreigners was transparent. Rachel did not expect to see any greater joy on her face until the day she came to know Christ as her Savior.

Akawo was immediately at home in the new clearing. She soon hung her hammock and reclined in it as she stirred the boiling pot on the fire within easy reach. She chattered contentedly with Rachel.

"You are Nimu. You came down from the sky. You must call me Mother." Akawo was pleased that her little girl's name had been given to Rachel by Dayuma.

The old mother quickly laid aside the outsiders' dress. Her only apparel was the costume jewelry Dayuma had brought her.

Although Akawo had heard Dayuma tell of God's carving and of how His Son came to earth, this information had brought little response. Her life continued almost as it had through the years.

As Rachel and Betty became a part of the Auca settlement, visiting and conversing with the women was a daily routine. After a few days with Akawo, Rachel wrote, "Yesterday I saw the first glimmer of light on Akawo's circumscribed horizon. I went over to visit and sat in one hammock while she, sitting in her own hammock, fed the dogs, parrots, and smaller birds, and cooked the dried corn on her little ground fire. Peeling the scorched husks down, she gripped the ears of corn with her toes, broke off the parched kernels, and ate them. We talked about common, everyday things—ancestors and spearings and the birds in the sky. Presently she looked up to the blue sky towering with white clouds and asked, 'Does God *owuka*—stay in His hammock—away up there in the sky?' Well, as far as I am concerned, she may think of His throne as a hammock. It is certainly the functional equivalent in this culture. Why not think of hammocks in the house God is thatching for them up there? But God's furnishings will surpass either the hammock or beautiful furniture and Oriental rugs."

Dayuma's younger sister Oba, her husband, Dyuwi, and their baby girl Adyibae, soon followed Akawo. "Oba has all the charm of the other girls," Rachel observed, "the same gracious smile and poise." Dyuwi had all but lost his life when the foreigners attacked the Aucas. A big gunshot scar was visible on his back.

Young Monga made an overnight visit. He was not as openly friendly as the others and kept eyeing the guns of the Quichua carriers who were still there when he came. He was pale and pathetic-looking and ill-at-ease. Very early in conversation with Rachel and Betty, he pointed out his spear wounds received downriver when his brother-in-law Kipa was killed. He made it plain that he had not gone along when the Aucas speared the five foreigners.

Uncle Gikita arrived next with his young boys Komi and Koni. Jolly and good-natured, Gikita talked to the foreign women with a snaggle-toothed grin. Although not aged, he was the patriarch of the group. Out of curiosity, he had come to see the visitors Dayuma had brought.

Dayuma's half brother Minkayi and his wife, Ompora, arrived a few days later. Rachel observed that "Minkayi is an extrovert. He is lanky and broad-shouldered. Friendly, he smiles most of the time.

"He made *pogantas*—crowns of palm fiber—and woven arm bands for us. I put them on and did a few of their galloping dance steps until Gimari just about collapsed laughing. I told Minkayi I wanted lightning bugs for the arm bands. Afterward, he said that when he went home he would catch a lot of toucan birds and make feather headbands for Betty and me."

Nimonga came later with his wife, Wiña, and her mother, Gami. Nimonga was short and stocky, and his dark and foreboding expression was accentuated by the black *huito* dye he had smeared on his face. Even the talk about his sister Wiñaemi and his sister-in-law Umi—both of whom still lived at the hacienda—did not seem to soften his evident dislike of the newcomers. However, old Gami, Dayuma's aunt, listened eagerly to news of her long-lost daughter, and her eyes filled with tears. She showed the foreigners the spear wounds she had received downriver when Wawae and Wamoñi were killed. It seemed natural for Auca conversation to center on spearings and scars.

The shelters on the Tiwaeno were ideal for observing Auca life and for hearing the language day and night. Without walls, they were actually no more than corner posts and a ridgepole supporting a palm-thatched roof.

Lessons in language and anthropology continued without interruption even after dark, as described by Rachel in a letter entitled "Night Life Among the Aucas":

"At dark everyone turns in—unless there is a pot of monkey meat on the fire, or bright moonlight, or rain that blows in the wall-less huts. Long-legged Uncle Gikita stretches out crosswise in his hammock, his huge bare feet hanging over the fire, sometimes pulling his little boy in on top of him. Little Tyaemae lies on her stomach in her hammock swung on the other side of the fire, and I can see her dainty little feet, toes down, in the lighted smoke of the fire. Maengamo burned her hammock before she went to the foreigners' houses last year, so she plunks down on another side of the fire on an old piece of a dugout canoe. Her teenage son swings his hammock high between the next two posts and curls his legs up. That leaves me to put down the bamboo boards, blow up an air mattress, hang a mosquito net, and enjoy both a blanket and the fire. Someone keeps the fire whipped up most of the night.

"When Dabu, Kimo's brother, came to visit, he slept on a piece of canoe under one of the hammocks. His long, tousled hair was not a foot and a half from mine. At 4:30 A.M. I had a nightmare and screamed loud enough for Dayuma to hear me in her nearby shelter.

" 'Nimu—Nimu!' she called, but the moans continued. 'Rachel!' she switched to English and woke me—and everyone else.

"Dabu sat bolt upright and said, 'Nimu, what is your name?'

" 'My mother calls me Rachel,' I said. From that moment on, Dabu and his sister Maengamo carried on an animated conversation about the foreigners' houses.

"Another night when the pups began to bark, Maengamo decided that the downriver group had come to attack. She hurried out to a big log and for fifteen minutes called out to the unseen foe: 'You all watch out! Don't spear us! The foreigners are with us here. We are learning about God and we want to live well.'

"Under the reciprocal law of the Aucas, these groups have accounts to settle. This, too, is an effective device of Satan for wiping out a heathen tribe before it ever hears of a Savior. Recently the downriver group did come looking for these Aucas, but their search was in vain though they came close to the old village where some of Dayuma's relatives still live. Our faith reaches out to the downriver group (a few of whom live with us here), but even Dayuma does not see how this dreaded foe could be reached for the Lord.

"Dayuma's dear old mother through the years has seen the spear-killing of her father, two sisters, a brother, husband, son, daughter, son-in-law, plus many other relatives. 'Sin when it is finished bringeth forth death.' It has brought much death here. Practically all of the men and some of the boys who live here on this clearing have taken part in spearings. And all—men, women, and children—have felt the effects of sin and its pattern, which were slowly wiping out this primitive tribe. May the standard of God 'whose we are and whom we serve' be raised against it."

Long after Rachel and Betty would retire for the night, Dayuma often talked around the glowing log fires with her people. Sometimes, however, there were interruptions in a night's slumber.

Rachel recalls, "One night after I was sound asleep I was awakened by Dayuma: 'Nimu! Minkayi says he wants to believe in the Lord!' Blessed interruption to a night's sleep. She had been talking to him at her mother's blazing fire as they swung in their hammocks. 'I told him Jesus is coming again someday and he must be ready to go with Him.'

" 'Fine,' I said. 'Now you must teach him more about who Jesus is.'

" 'I did—I told him how He was born, how He lived, how He died, and how He was raised again....' Thank God for this open heart.

"Back to sleep. Then the soft pattering of bare feet.

" 'Nimu!' and a proffered gift of monkey meat from Ompora. Another blessed interruption, an acceptable sign of friendship and interest. Minkayi had killed the monkey with his blowgun.

"Asleep again—and called once again.

" 'Nimu!' I sat up, and without a word Nimonga's wife, Wiña, handed me a cooked monkey leg, hairs half burned off, skin and toenails on! Without a word, I took it and thanked the Lord for this further sign of friendship on the part of one who had seemed so unfriendly.

"The night's sleep was further interrupted when Maengamo sat up in the dark (as she often does) and began to sing the strong nasal chants of the tribe. Nor do I fully understand the motives and emotions that prompt them—anything from war cries to pretty little songs about the birds. Someday there will be songs of praises to the living God rising as a sweet savor to Him during the long hours of the night....

"They say the very best way to learn a language with the proper intonation is to hear it subconsciously, even when one is doing something else. This night life ought to do something for me. I rejoice at the opportunity to hear the Auca language the last thing at night, the first thing in the morning, and many hours in between....

"There is a rhythm and melody to this language that Dayuma has lost through the years outside the tribe. One of my favorite sports is trying to imitate it, which sends Dayuma's sisters into gales of laughter. Nothing ventured, nothing gained!"

As the foreigners settled in to Auca living, they learned to eat, as well as speak, with the forest people. "The more men there are here, the better the food supply," wrote Rachel. Monkeys and birds were blowgunned in quantity when several men were on the clearing, and fish were speared in the river. Some fish were hand-caught in the nearby streams by women and children. Sometimes Rachel and Betty were invited by the Aucas to go hunting wild hogs or other animals in the forest.

One day Gikita's son Kimo came back to the clearing and announced that he had killed an *amunga* monkey carrying its young. But alas, the prize had fallen into the hollow center of a high tree. He was recruiting help to fell the tree and extract the monkey. Dayuma invited Rachel to join the fun. Soon the group of young hunters along with Dayuma and Rachel were off to the forest. Wato, the youngest girl of the expedition, carried embers for making smoke to ward off the swarms of insects that were sure to attack unprotected bodies.

When they arrived at the tree where the monkey had fallen, the boys surveyed the situation first and chopped down several smaller trees to make a clearing through which the huge tree could fall to the ground. The young Indians took turns with the ax, and finally the giant of the forest crashed to the ground and the woodsmen retrieved the monkey. To their delight, they found two porcupines inhabiting the same hollow trunk. Although the attempt to smoke them out failed, the effort was great sport. Swarms of bees molested the party, but Wato and Dayuma drove most of them off with their smudge. They found the beehive in a small tree nearby. After the search for the porcupines was abandoned, the small tree was felled, the bees smoked out, and honey enjoyed by all.

On another occasion the lively Tiwaeno young people went to the forest for a honey feast. They felled a big *wipita* tree which held a huge hive. When the tree hit the ground, the enthusiastic Aucas dug into the honey with their hands, scooped up the exotic jungle nectar and, licking their fingers and smacking loudly, consumed as much as they could of the sticky delicacy.

When the Indians had eaten their fill, they dipped gourd bowls into the honey to be carried home for the older folks and children. They also chipped off pieces of the colorful *wipita* wood to make medicine for foot itch or to be used for extracting dark red dye for fishing nets and hammocks. The heart of the fresh-hewn tree was a glowing deep-rose color.

For the foreigners, living with the forest people was a liberal education in adaptation to one's environment. The ingenious tribespeople fully exploited the forest not only for food, but also for many other useful commodities. Supplies from cultivated crops still came from the former clearing. Bananas and yuca were brought by the women and girls over the rugged trail in heavy-laden baskets resting against their backs and supported by bark tumplines across their foreheads. Crops were well under way on the Tiwaeno, however, and as the forest was cleared, more yuca was planted.

From time to time there were special gifts of food from members of the family wanting to express their satisfaction with the new settlers. Rachel wrote of Dabu's trip to the Tiwaeno several weeks after his first visit:

"Dabu, tall and broad-chested, arrived last night with a gift for his cousin Dayuma, a huge basketful of smoked wild hog which he had carried all day over a rough and steep trail. Dabu lives further away than any of Dayuma's relatives. He had been to visit us only once before. From the first, he seemed impressed with the fact that we had come to tell the Aucas about God. The MAF plane was due to make a supply flight, so Dabu decided to stay over a day and see it again. It has been three years now since he first saw that little yellow plane piloted by Nate....

"Toña, a young Auca lad from downriver, came with Dabu. This was his second visit. How well I remember the first one. His young

face, with the thin and handsome straighter features of the downriver group, had been filled with sadness, seriousness, and down-
right fear of us. He had sat down on a log and refused to come near.

"This time he evidently set aside his fears, and went all out to
see what the foreigners were like. All morning he watched us write,
cook, and swim, and he listened to us trying to talk his language. He
said nothing until he could contain himself no longer, then he
threw back his head, laughed heartily, and said something about me
I simply could not understand.

" 'What did you say, Toña?' I said. 'I just don't hear.'

"With that he repeated something, laughing uproariously,
which made it still harder to understand. But I was determined. I
came closer and asked him to tell me slowly. Then all the Aucas
went into gales of laughter. I finally gave up, wrote what I had
caught of it in my notebook, and found out later what he had said.
Then it was my turn to laugh.

" 'Nimu, if you just had your hair cut in bangs over your ears,
you would be able to hear us!' had been Toña's comment.

"Traditional hairstyle here (cut with sharp clam shells) for men
and women, young and old alike, calls for bangs halfway around the
head to a point behind the ears. This makes a pretty frame for the
balsa earplugs, leaving the ears free to hear the Auca language
clearly. But it will take a lot more than an Auca haircut to enable me
to understand all I hear in this Auca clearing."

As Dayuma readapted quickly to the forest, she took her place
clearing weeds for crops, planting yuca, bringing firewood, or
spearing fish. Consequently, there is no such thing as regular hours
for either study or teaching. "It just doesn't work out that way,"
Rachel wrote. "As for teaching her the Word, or reviewing with her a
lesson for the coming Sunday, I just have to take whatever opportunities that come, when the others have gone off to fish or swim and
she is more or less alone." Although Dayuma did gather her people
together on Sunday mornings for a very informal time of instruction in God's carving, most of her teaching was offhand and
unscheduled. Rachel tells of such a lesson during Dabu's visit:

"Early in the morning after Dabu's sister Maengamo and some
of the others had gone off to clear the forest for planting, Dayuma

began to tell Dabu about God's Son, Jesus. We were all sitting around the ground fire on 'pews' made of old split canoes. I watched Dabu as he sat shaving darts for his blowgun, scarcely ever looking up at Dayuma. Was he listening? It was hard to tell. I noted the ways Dayuma sought to make the story clear.

" 'The foreigners were watching their "pets" at night—pets, something like deer,' she began, trying to describe sheep for an Auca who had never seen one. Then she went on telling him of the birth of Jesus.

" 'Those watching their pets said, "Let's go fast to see." Then they came to a tiny thatched hut where Joseph and Mary were—'

" 'Was He already born?' interrupted Dabu. How well he had been following every word! Dayuma finished her story with a brief résumé of Jesus' life, death, and resurrection.

"In conclusion, she said to her cousin, 'Now, Dabu, you teach this same thing to your children.'

" 'I shall teach my children,' Dabu replied."

Dayuma was grateful that her people were listening well to her now, without laughing as they had at first. Gradually, they began to understand why the five foreign men had come to the Curaray, and now the two foreign women with Dayuma.

"Not understanding, we killed your men," some said, and others added, "Now we will hear from God." Each week Dayuma gathered her little brood under a thatched roof and taught them God's carving.

Rachel relates, "First Dayuma instructs them not to laugh, then she teaches them little by little about God, the Creator, and His Son, Jesus. In telling of Jairus's daughter the other day, she explained, 'When someone dies in the foreigners' houses, they cry. They don't laugh as the Aucas do'—and then she proceeded with the story. As she prays, she asks the Lord to throw out the witch doctors and the devils. Tyaenyae, the mother of Wiñaemi, the youngest Auca girl still living at the hacienda, is known as a witch doctor here. (She hasn't come to see us yet.) Whenever someone is sick, they say she has bewitched that person, and threaten to spear her if he dies."

On October 12, Rachel noted a meeting typical of those early gatherings in the clearing:

"Today I had the joy of hearing Dayuma teach God's Word to all the Aucas on the Tiwaeno clearing. Nimonga sent little Ana to call me, then they called all the Aucas together in mother Akawo's hut.

" 'Sit there on the log—or over here,' directed Dayuma as the informal meeting got under way.

"Dayuma called again to the others in their huts, and finally all came to hear. She chose to tell the story of Joseph. The young Aucas laughed, but all of the others listened well. After she had Joseph's bones ordered back to his father's land, she told her people to shut their eyes, that she was going to talk to God. She prayed for her people, that they would come to know Him so that when He returned and called they would 'following Him go up to heaven.' She prayed for Mother and Dad, and for Betty's folks, and for Sammy in school in Quito. She prayed for those who are leaving to go downriver today, that the snakes would not bite them. She prayed that Jesus would command the devils to go out of the bodies of the Aucas, and that they would live well. When she prayed, there was not a sound out of anyone—all were respectful, although they had seemed a bit embarrassed at the story."

On another Sunday, Dayuma told of the birth of Christ which Rachel had reviewed with her during the week. Rachel noted, "She even included the fact that Joseph was of the house of David—a detail that I hadn't mentioned for weeks. The Lord certainly has blessed her with a keen memory, and the Holy Spirit seems to bring things to her remembrance.... Omaenkiri, one of Uncle Gikita's wives, didn't seem to pay much attention, nor the young girls. The young boys saw a bird in the forest and interrupted the story a bit. There were other interruptions, too, but all in all the meeting went well. Then Dayuma prayed: 'All close your eyes now, we're going to talk to God. Keep Uncle Gikita and the others on the trail. Don't let the snakes bite them. Throw out the witch doctors and the devils. Who will be the first to love and obey God and live well?' "

As Rachel listened to Dayuma teaching her people about God and His Son, she marveled that "in God's planning, Dayuma was the first one to carry the name of Jesus to her people." Three years before when she began to teach Dayuma at Hacienda Ila, no one in the Auca forest knew His name. Now in telling Bible stories, Dayuma would begin her narration in good Auca fashion by first introducing the name of the main character: "Jesus, His name is Jesus...." Gradually, her people were learning His name.

Omaenkiri, Gikita's wife and sister of Naenkiwi, was the first of the older generation to respond to the teaching about God's Son. In making her daily rounds, Rachel often visited Omaenkiri in her separate thatched hut.

Rachel recorded, "Omaenkiri's mother Dyiko came over the trail to visit us. She and her other daughter Nombo came with the rest of the Aucas out of curiosity to see the foreigners. One day when I arrived in Omaenkiri's hut, old Grandmother Dyiko was nursing her grandchild. Squatting beside her, her daughter Nombo also was nursing her baby.

"That day as Omaenkiri sat in her hammock with her little children, stirring up her fire and talking to her mother and sister, she began to tell them that I had come with Dayuma to teach them about Jesus. It was a big thrill for me to listen to Omaenkiri telling her family what Dayuma had taught her about the birth of Christ. I was amazed at the details she remembered. But as she told the story, she turned to me and said, 'Now what was His name?' The name of Jesus was strange to her, and she couldn't remember it. Suddenly it occurred to me that I was now hearing an Auca from the forest itself—not Dayuma—telling still other Aucas about Jesus!

"Shortly after I heard her tell the story, Omaenkiri came down with the fever and colds that had been going around since the initial contact with the outside. But carrying one little child and leading another, she had left on the trail to go back to her home.

"A day or two later Monga, his body wet with the recent rain, appeared on the other side of our little river before the sun was very high in the sky. All of the Aucas knew that he was a bearer of 'ill tidings.' Only one who had run all the way over the jungle trail could have arrived at that hour. The message, which he breathlessly called out across the stream, was for Uncle Gikita, who was tying palm leaves with vines to the framework over our heads."

Omaenkiri, Gikita's wife, was dying. "Tell my husband to come quickly. Who will bury my dead body?" was the message. Monga, who was from downriver, distrusted everyone—his own people as well as the foreign women toward whom he had been hostile on his first visit to the Tiwaeno.

Gikita finally persuaded Monga to cross the river and give a few details. Then Gikita shinnied down the bamboo post, picked a few green bananas out of a basket, and prepared to leave immediately. Betty and Rachel wondered if either of them should go to help the sick mother, but it seemed out of the question to do more than send some pills with Gikita.

As he set off on the trail with Monga, Dayuma called after her uncle, "If Omaenkiri dies, don't choke the baby! God doesn't want us to do that. Let the baby live!"

Several days later the Indian women returned with their heavy loads of yuca and bananas, and the word that Omaenkiri had died. But her baby had not been choked. Her niece Wato, a bashful young girl once rescued by Uncle Gikita after she had wandered alone for weeks in the forest, stated the facts of her aunt's death without the faintest semblance of sadness. Maengamo gave more details. Dayuma alone, her heart softened by love for the Lord, wept openly as she swung in the hammock and listened.

On the way home, Omaenkiri had felt a hard blow on the back of her head. Her son denied dealing it. From that moment on, she was sure the devils had hit her and she would die. Later, when the fever had taken its full toll and coughs wracked her body, she ran outside from her hammock, crying, "Mima is calling me—I must go!"—and fell dead.

Omaenkiri's little children were a part of the family on the Tiwaeno. One day, Rachel noted that "the three children had their fire burning merrily at 5:30 A.M., and seemed perfectly capable of carrying on without their mother." Widows and orphans found their niche in group life, and each did his share of work by hunting, fishing, or clearing weeds in the yuca patch.

Dayuma and Gimari, both widows themselves, sometimes fished together. "During her first days on the Tiwaeno," Rachel relates, "Dayuma had still felt some resentment toward Gimari for the way she had gone off with Naenkiwi, causing such heartache to the family. Upon her first arrival at the Tiwaeno, when she greeted

Gimari she had not even asked the name of her baby. Gradually, forgiveness replaced Dayuma's initial anger."

Although Gimari no longer laughed at Dayuma's teaching, there was no spark of curiosity either. As Rachel tried to make friends with Gimari, though, she began to see in her the same possibilities there had been in Dayuma. "After a little while," Rachel recalls, "in spite of herself Gimari began to listen. I started teaching her as I had Dayuma, line upon line, precept upon precept, very simple truths. Finally, I got her to respond to questions. At first she would whisper the answer very quietly.

" 'Gimari, where does God live?' and she would point up to the sky in her bashfulness.

" 'How many sons does He have?'

" '*Aroki*—just one,' she whispered.

" 'What is His Son's name?'

" 'His Son's name—I don't remember,' Gimari said softly.

"I taught her the name of Jesus over and over again until she could remember it. Then to my great joy, I found that Gimari would not only whisper His name, but she was also teaching baby Bai the name of the Son of God. In fact, Jesus was one of the first words that baby Bai lisped."

In that name lay the hope that Bai would not grow up to avenge the spearing of his father Naenkiwi.

# CHAPTER EIGHTEEN

# "Just Like Kapok, Rising with the Wind"

$A$s the Explorer VII streaked through space and settled into orbit in the autumn of 1959, another conquest was in progress on a tiny clearing back on the earth's surface. Occupation of the Auca settlement by the bearers of good tidings for earth dwellers had been quiet and unspectacular. But like the launching of the rocket, it was a historical incident.

"You are making history here on earth—and in eternity," wrote one interested friend to Rachel.

"If we are," was her response, "the Lord has chosen this tiny spot to highlight for the world many tribes being reached by missionaries, unseen and unsung, too busy with the job at hand to write home about it...."

For those who had hoped and prayed for many years that the isolated tribe of the forest would be won for Christ, the Auca advance was victory in a new dimension. Fear of foreigners, the chief obstacle to progress, was being overcome by the love of God through human channels. Dayuma, who now taught her people God's carving, oriented them also in their relation to a larger world. She was drawing aside the forest curtain.

As her people stood around in their natural nakedness or in various stages of dress, Dayuma told them about the rest of the world. She wore a cotton print dress which she had made herself, but for Aucas in general, the wearing of clothing was still a custom of outsiders.

"Our Auca country is like a drop of spit on the back of my hand," she said to them, realistically matching action with her words. "The land is small; the water is very, very big. The land is like this"—she picked up a gourd bowl, turned it upside down, and pointed to the imaginary continents—"and all *this* part is water." The improvised world globe was amusing to some and incredible to others, but at least the rudiments of physical geography had been taught.

The foreign women were closely observed in their first months on the Tiwaeno. From the time of their grandfathers, the Aucas had referred to such people as "like *bogi* monkeys" whose palms are white. With only one Auca word for "outsider," it was convenient to compare the white foreigners to the well-known monkey. Rachel was called a "red-skin" because of her fair, sunburned skin upon arrival at the settlement. To the dark-eyed Aucas, the blue eyes of the foreigners were "like rain." And the foreigners spoke their queer language "with crooked teeth," or with "a dry tongue."

In spite of the resistance of a few, there was a heartening reaction of several to the new way of life. From the beginning, Dawa had been eager to hear, but at times the things taught by Dayuma and reiterated by Rachel seemed incredible. One day when the lesson had been about Jesus' walking on the water "just as if it were beach," Dawa objected.

"That couldn't be—no man can walk on water!"

"But Jesus *did*," Dayuma insisted. "He is the Son of God—He *made* the water, and He walked on it." Dawa began to accept the teaching concerning the miracles of Christ as she realized that He was the Ruler of all nature.

Lessons taught in the daytime were often continued at night around the fires or in the hammocks. As the Aucas reviewed the amazing truths of God's carving, the foreign women absorbed more of the language of the forest. At that time Rachel wrote, "I asked the

Lord for that which would help me most with the language, and I guess I got it. Maengamo's open-air hut, with Ipa and baby Tamaenta, is a perfect setup for learning Auca. And the fire where the meat is smoked is a comfort as it dries the damp bedding...."

Pet monkeys rustled the palm leaves overhead at night, and tame birds stirred on their roosts. Occasionally, a sudden, pitiful cry signaled the distress of a night victim. Once when Rachel was awakened by the half-human cry of a suffering animal, she woke Dayuma and asked what it was. At first Dayuma said it was just a jaguar killing a *paenae*. But as she listened to the prolonged cry, she said no, it was a boa attacking its prey. "If it squeals a long time, a boa is crushing it," she explained.

During the day, pets were a source of amusement—and sometimes consternation—to Rachel. She laughed when Dayuma's monkey grabbed a banana from the pet parrot, but a little while later the picture changed. Unnoticed, the thief sneaked down the rafter and snatched away a cooked bird thigh that Rachel was about to eat. Then, after devouring the juicy morsel in front of Rachel, it ran high up in the peak of the roof.

Sometimes the "juicy morsel" was a relative of the pet *iwa* monkey itself. "The *gamunga* monkey is peeking out of the pot, head and torso," Rachel wrote as she observed a meal in the making. "I have really gone into neutral on such things. I believe I could even eat a monkey head now—though I wouldn't want to deprive the Aucas of a delicacy. The smoked ones still remind me of the shrunken heads of Tariri's tribe."

Once in a while when monkey hunting had been good, there was a feast of monkey heads. All ate to the full of the delicious meat as soon as it was cooked, but the heads were saved for the next day's feast. Mother Akawo would pass out the delicacies, the largest heads being given to the oldest men, and the smallest to baby Bai. As they squatted on the ground around the fire, they would noisily lick and suck the skulls. It was a unique experience for a foreigner, and something of a psychological adjustment to food fashions.

One day Oba arrived with a collection of charred monkey limbs poking out the top of a basket. She presented Rachel with "all the appendages as a very special gift, topped by two blackened monkey heads. I am getting over some of my prejudices. I finally consumed some of the brains myself, but left the sucking of the eyes to Akawo."

As Christmas approached, a brief recess on the outside was suggested. Dayuma desperately wanted to visit her son, Sammy. Jim Elliot's parents would be coming to South America, and Betty was eager to see them. So Rachel and Betty packed a few belongings and made their way with Auca companions through the forest and up the rivers to Arajuno. They came out as quietly as they had gone in. Their first stay of almost two months in the Auca settlement was brimming with rich experiences. If the Aucas had learned much, the foreign women had learned more.

Rachel and Dayuma took Sammy to Quito for the holidays. While there, they entertained a special visitor. Miss Marguerite Carter of Gospel Recordings, Inc., in California had come to Ecuador to help make records in the Auca language to be played later for Dayuma's people in the forest. By diligent work and with Dayuma's cooperation, material for four records was successfully taped. Each of the records, three minutes on each side, contained in concentrated Auca a succinct summary of Scripture stories. Two of the records were prepared from material taped as Dayuma had first taught Mintaka and Maengamo about God. The content of the four records would give an uninitiated Auca a fair idea of what God's carving said, from the creation of the world to the death and resurrection of Christ. The tapes were flown to Los Angeles to be processed and then pressed into records.

In late February, Dayuma and Rachel returned to the tribe. Betty and Valerie were delayed and would follow in March. The trip in alone with Dayuma was an intensive lesson in jungle travel for Rachel—with an experienced private guide. As they left their Quichua carrier at Tapir River, Dayuma put Rachel in the lead on the trail. It was time she learned the ways of the woods. But in the virgin Auca forest, Rachel would stray and follow the path of the tapir or deer. Dayuma would then laugh or even scold, "Can't you see where the Aucas have bent the sticks on their trail?" Bent or broken twigs and sticks had to be recognized. And Dayuma cautioned Rachel against snakes. The leader on the trail always kept his eyes peeled for them.

Finally, after arriving and settling again, Rachel wrote on February 20, "Dayuma and I came over the trail carrying a minimum of equipment. We knew before we arrived that there would not be many Indians around. Dayuma's forest-trained eyes had failed to find footprints, and the trails were overgrown. They had to be opened up, though we had been gone such a short time. There was no one on the clearing when we arrived, but the logs were still glowing in Kimo's hut. Soon Dawa, followed by her pet wild hog, came splashing across the river in response to our call.

"This was the second time that Kimo and Dawa had waited for the foreigners. The first time the others had waited awhile, and then left when their long-established fears of foreigners got the better of them. This time, when the new moon appeared and we had not returned, the witch doctor began the refrain that the foreigners will not return. But Kimo waited—Kimo who just three years before had gone with the others to kill the five foreign men on the Curaray.

"At twilight Kimo came back from hunting, poison-dart holder swung around his neck, blowgun and fishing spear over his shoulder, but alas—empty-handed. Kimo hung up his dart holder, carefully slipped his blowgun across the thatch in its accustomed place, sat down in the hammock, and warmed himself by the fire in the tiny shack. He drank the ripe banana drink his wife offered him in a gourd. Then, as the sun sank behind the high trees, he and Dayuma started to talk:

" 'Nimonga and Monga said you wouldn't come,' Kimo began. 'Dreaming, your mother saw you come back with Nimu.... Omaenkiri's baby is so thin.... Boika's new baby was a girl. She wanted to step on it and kill it.... Returning, Uncle Gikita will bring Maengamo at the next full moon.... Dabu is planting a new yuca patch downriver. Later, bringing his food by canoe, he will live with us here.... Returning from the foreigners' houses, everyone was sick....'

"Soon it was Dayuma's turn: 'The Quichua carriers who brought us were old and tired. They brought our things to Tapir River and returned.... We heard that the downriver Indians killed a foreigner over on the big river, and lots of foreigners went looking for them with guns—foreigners who don't love the Lord.... Gikari [the Auca name given to Betty Elliot] and her little girl will be coming later—we came first because we didn't want to keep you waiting any longer.... We saw a big anteater on the trail.... Did you know we would be coming when our wood-bee flew over? The man in the wood-bee thought you were Dabu....'

"'Did He?' asked Kimo. 'The wood-bee just went round and round. We heard it coming—*wuu, wuu, wuu*—and then it went round and round.... Who is his wife, the wood-bee man? How many children does he have?... No, we haven't killed anyone since you left. We have not been over to the Curaray.... Tomorrow, I will go to Tapir River and pick up your things. Alone I will go the next day over the trail to your mother and the others. I will tell them you are back....'"

Twilight turned to darkness, moonbeams filled the open shelter, stars became brighter. Soon the conversation faded with the dying fires as they all fell asleep.

Before Kimo left for the family clearing downriver, he and Dawa were speculating with Dayuma about the others. "Why haven't they come? Who would tell us if the downriver Indians had speared them all?" Later Dayuma informed Rachel of the predictions: The enemy would take her half-sister Ana, and she would become the wife of a downriver man. Bai would be killed because he is a small boy. Adyibae would be speared because her mother, Oba, couldn't escape with her; Dyuwi, because he is a man; and Mother Akawo, because she is old.

It was a grim picture Dayuma and Kimo painted, and Rachel prayed that someone might come soon with word.

Several days later at twilight, Rachel heard the glad shout, "Kimo has returned!" Again, Kimo warmed himself at the fire and pulled his strong, muscular legs up in the hammock beside Dawa as he told the news.

"Your sister Gimari is sick. She almost died, but she is better now. Akawo told baby Bai that if his mother died, she would hit him over the head and kill him. She said she would put him in the hole with Gimari. Then little Bai cried and cried...."

Rachel was shocked. She knew of Akawo's threat to kill Dayuma when she was a small child if Moipa speared her father. But baby Bai was so small—he could barely say a few words.

"All of them were very sick," Kimo continued. "They are better now. Uncle Gikita nearly died with bad skin sores. He said he was bewitched by the Quichua Indians when he went to the outside. He saw a fellow with 'rotted feet' in their village, and said he was cursed in the same way. He was so sick he sent for Dyuwi to come and bury him. Akawo had a sore toe and couldn't go over the trail to see him. Gami went, but she wasn't much help. When he was almost gone—he was so weak he couldn't talk—Maengamo made a paste of hot peppers and rubbed it on his sores. That really brought him to. It burned so much that he rallied. Gami gave him hot water mixed with something else, and he began to get better.

"All of them were angry at Dayuma—even Akawo—for bringing in the sicknesses from the outside. Two have already died, Mima and Omaenkiri, and now these sicknesses. Nimonga said he would spear us all if Gikita died."

"Who—me?" asked Rachel.

"Yes."

"And you, Kimo?"

"Yes."

"And Gikari—and her little girl?"

"Yes."

"And Maengamo?"

"No…"

Then Kimo recited more family calamities:

"Minkayi was bitten by a stingray and nearly died. His mother said she would bury one of his children with him if he died. He is better now…. Mintaka has gone to live with Nimonga…. Maengamo said the bugs were bad here on the Tiwaeno. She has built another hut downriver…."

One day Rachel heard Dayuma teaching Dawa about God's carving—a welcome relief from the sad family news volleyed repeatedly from hammock to hammock. She said of Adam and Eve, "If they hadn't sinned, we wouldn't get sick and die—and we wouldn't have to clear weeds now. You see how it is when we are gone only a short time. We have to cut through the trail in places. God said to Adam, 'Adam, clearing weeds and planting yuca stalks you will live.'"

Later, Dawa was overheard relaying a lesson to Kimo. "God created *everything*.... We know the names of two stars, *gagai*—'evening star'—and *wanimu*—'morning star,' but God knows the names of all the stars."

It was evident that Dawa pondered well all that she heard.

"Dawa does a lot of thinking," Dayuma said. "She isn't like the others. Laughing, Kimo says, 'Before, we used to eat dirty. Now that Dayuma has taught you, you have listened.'" And Dayuma added, "Now Dawa keeps her hut clean. Being careful, she serves the food."

⮾ ⮾ ⮾ ⮾

By the first week in March when Betty and Valerie rejoined the Tiwaeno family, none of the Aucas from downriver had yet returned. It was a desolate scene, compared with the vibrant activity a few months before. But a week later, Akawo finally arrived with Dyuwi and Oba and little Adyibae, and Maengamo appeared with Tyaemae and Wato. The clearing soon began to echo once again with the merry laughter of young voices and the friendly chatter of older women.

And once again there were joyful expeditions into the forest. One day the Aucas and foreigners went in search of delicious *awaemae* fruit growing high in the big trees. When they located a fruit tree, Kimo quickly wrapped a strong jungle vine five times around his ankles in a support for shinnying up the tree.

Kimo soon pulled himself to a height of about 150 feet. He clung to the trunk of the tree, barely reaching around it. Then, machete in hand, he started lopping off the branches which held the tasty fruit and tossing them to the ground for Dayuma and Rachel to place in the palm-leaf baskets they had made. Between strokes, he picked the fruit and ate as fast as he could. Then Kimo slithered gracefully down the trunk.

Another day while traveling alone in the forest, Kimo saw a huge boa. He was without his weapons, but heaved stones at it to stun it. Then he returned home for his machete and spears. Rachel wrote:

"We followed Kimo on the trail and saw the immense ugly creature, almost twenty feet long. Kimo first speared its head, and we watched the contraction of its strong muscles as it slowly wrapped its body around the spear. Then he and Dayuma quickly made more rough chonta spears and jabbed the creature, pinning it to the streambed to which it had slithered. Kimo speared again, and all watched and yelled as the boa wound around the spear. They jabbed it several more times, then he and Dayuma began pulling the spears out and re-jabbing until the stream flowed red with blood. Finally, when they had pulled all the spears out, the beast stretched itself in fury to its full length and advanced, mouth open and head up. With a mighty yell, Kimo speared it right down the throat.

"I was so impressed with the strength of the boa—you could see it in the tightening of the muscles. The spearing technique made me shaky as I watched; people were killed by the Aucas in just this same way."

Sometimes there were fishing sprees, or a wild hog chase. As other young Aucas from the former clearing joined the group, the activities were pursued with greater spirit. One afternoon a simple fishing trip turned out to be a greater success than anticipated. The Indians encountered a herd of hogs at the edge of the river, and immediately gave chase. Young Kinta speared one. It was probably his first wild hog. Rachel says, "He was one proud little boy as he climbed up the bank with a big smile, his white teeth shining in the afternoon sun." Fortunately, they had taken the canoe to spear fish, so it was a simple matter to dump all the fish and hogs in the canoe and bring it home.

The extra food supply gave Dayuma the opportunity to call them all together to begin the long-envisioned clearing of an airstrip on the Tiwaeno. There were huge trees to be felled, and heavy stumps to hack and heave and haul away—but Dayuma inspired her people to tackle the tremendous task.

Little Bai carried off the first root to clear the strip. Rachel remembered that her brother Nate had tried to tell Bai's father Naenkiwi—or "George" as he called him—that he wanted a strip made. "God's ways are past finding out," she wrote in her diary, "but we have had the privilege of seeing the little son actually start it."

One day when the work was barely under way, a plane was heard overhead. An impressive group of Aucas waved greetings to the large plane of the Ecuadorian Air Force on its way east to the border. The plane made a turn and circled back over the Auca field.

"Look!" shouted Dayuma. "Flying low, the big wood-bee of the chief of the land comes to see! All hands to work!"

On the same exciting day, the JAARS plane flew over unannounced on its way back to the Limoncocha base. Still later that day, the MAF plane passed overhead unexpectedly on its way home to Shell Mera. After a while the government plane circled again on its way back to Quito. There was almost too much excitement for one day, but it gave impetus to the airstrip project.

After each day's work, the Aucas relaxed in the hammocks around the fires, where they swapped stories or sang. The exotic songfests are described by Rachel:

"As the daylight fades and the moon rises in the east, the Aucas pull their feet up into their hammocks, or stretch them out over the dying embers of the burning logs of the fire nearby. Then one or another of the men will break out in the rhythmic, nasalized, oft-repeated stanzas of an Auca song. Perhaps it should more aptly be called chanting, but whatever it is I have come to enjoy it. Sometimes a grandmother will sing as her grandchild tugs at her breast. Sometimes several sing all at once—each a different song. That really adds to the effect. The seven huts in this clearing are mighty close together.

"At dawn it is often the same thing. I never know which will wake me up first: the rooster that was dropped as a little chick in a bucket by Nate, or Kimo or Dyuwi. Their hammocks are not twenty feet away, though they each have separate thatched roofs. The songs may be anything from 'I have worked hard all day like a leaf-cutting ant,' to a little ditty about 'Floating, floating in our new canoe.'"

As Aucas joined the settlement, the songs became more varied and frequent, and the volume greater.

By April, when all of Dayuma's family had arrived on the Tiwaeno clearing, those who had been hostile were more tolerant, even friendly. "Dyuwi is visibly softening toward us," Rachel observed. "Occasionally, he is actually hilarious about my attempts to imitate his wife's speech. He used to be sullen, so I am delighted to be laughed at. But we still have our problem child Monga, who tells so many lies it's hard to keep the picture straight. I think he is trying to be a 'big shot' and make up for the fact that he is an out-sider. Dayuma has 'lectured' him about 'talking wild.' Both Nimonga and Minkayi seem to have gotten over any fears they had.

"Dawa and Gimari are wanting to know more of the Lord. Last night Dawa got out of her hammock to sit up and listen to Dayuma telling a Bible story back to me after dark. In fact, from the comments coming from different directions, I judge there must have been at least a half dozen other listeners in various hammocks. Then Dawa prayed aloud to the Lord.

"A few do not come to the Sunday gatherings, but we are encouraged as we see the answers to prayer here and the general response."

As Easter approached, Dayuma drilled her family class on the death and resurrection of Christ. The story of the raising of His dead body had never ceased to thrill her, and she emphasized it to her people, most of whom were still fearful of what would happen to dead bodies.

Gimari and Dawa listened attentively as Dayuma's animation carried her audience along with her. They hung on every word.

"Then the followers of Jesus came and looked into the tomb—"

"*Ndae!*—There was no one!" shouted Dawa, her eyes shining with triumph. Dayuma beamed her approval, then continued with the sequel of the disciples' walk to Emmaus with the risen Christ.

"They two returned fast at night. They called out to the others, 'We have already seen Him. He is awake. We came back to tell you. He spoke to God—He is alive! We saw Him!'

"Then the others said, 'You must be talking wild. How can those who have already died be raised?'

"Then the two said, 'Why don't you understand? It is true what they said about Him long ago. They said He would live again.' Then another said, 'One moon and one-half moon He lived there, being raised.'

"Afterward He went high up in the sky. 'Now I will go away,' He said, 'and when I go away, I will go to be beside My Father, God. Now I am going up. Afterward, in the same way, returning I will come,' He said.

"He will come again, not as a child. He will come again in the same way He went—as a Man. You say that kapok being light goes up? Like that He went up, just like kapok, rising with the wind. Higher, higher, higher. Just like that. Going up, the wind takes the white fluff higher—like that, He went up. Up to the other side of the pretty clouds. Then He was not. Where did He go? They didn't see.

"Then the ones God sent, the ones who live high in the sky with God, came. 'Why do you all stay looking?' they said. 'You all in the same way will go up.' When will Jesus come? He is the One who said, 'After I go up high, I am going to come again.' Those who died long ago, believing in God, Jesus will call. Hearing, fast they will be raised. All of them, those who believed in God, will go high up in the sky.

"Now we do not know just when He will come. Day, night, sunset, midnight, dawn—we don't know. But He will come. When God says to His Son, 'Yes, now You go,' fast He will come.

"All of those who do not believe in God, all of them will be thrown out. You throw worms out of the corn. Like that God will throw them out. Do you all understand? That's how it is. Those who do not believe, the devil will take. It will be bad for all of them.

"That is how God's trail is—like that ravine over there on the other side of the river. You won't be able to cross over. Here is the devil's trail, and there is God's trail. It is a very, very beautiful trail as you go up there."

On Easter Sunday, Dayuma reviewed the story. Then she challenged them directly, "Who, and who, and who will say, 'Yes, I love God, I want to live well.' Dawa, will you?"

"Yes," said Dawa.

"Kimo?"

No reply.

"Gimari, will you?"

To her expression of consent, Gimari added, "*Tomamoni!*—All of us!"

Dayuma explained that those who love God often sing to Him in remembrance of good things He has done. One refrain in an old Auca song about the God of creation would be appropriate. Thus the simple gathering ended with the Auca chant, "God created, God created everything." Then, as if inspired by her own message concerning a risen Lord, Dayuma added original Auca words to the old tune:

*We say the stars shine, He created all…*
*Seeing, we will love Him in our hearts…*
*Following Jesus, to God's house we will go…*
*We will say "No" to the devils, we all will love God.*

Old and young quietly followed Dayuma's lead as each line was repeated many times.

Rachel wrote in her diary, "It was the very first 'congregational singing' in Auca! I'm sure it rejoiced the heart of the Lord who heard from heaven. May it be true that 'all of us' will believe in Him before another Easter Sunday in Aucaland."

CHAPTER NINETEEN

# "Our Ancestors
# Were Talking Wild"

Old Akawo sat in her hammock, rolling the strands of *chambira* fiber against her bare thigh with her wrinkled hand. At times as she chanted an Auca tune or called to her grandchildren as they played in the clearing, she would look down the path toward the stream. Two moons had passed since Dayuma and Rachel returned to the outside.

"Will Dayuma bring her son or not when she comes with Nimu?... Will he look like an Auca?..."

Her family did not really believe Dayuma had a son until Dabu went once to Arajuno and saw Sammy with his own eyes. Ever since then the others—especially his grandmother—had been eager to see him.

Finally, the big day arrived and the glad shout, "They have come!" rang through the Tiwaeno clearing. Akawo hastily pulled on her dress and waited in her hammock to welcome her family.

Sammy looked from one to another as Dayuma, speaking to him in Quichua, explained who his relatives were. Akawo was grinning from ear to ear.

"My grandchild he is!" Akawo could hardly believe her eyes. "He looks like Wawae."

Dika and Gingata looked Sammy over and decided he would be a good playmate, even though he spoke very few words of their language. For Akawo, lack of a common tongue was no barrier. From the moment she saw Sammy, she chattered with him in Auca, which she assumed he understood.

Sammy, who was immediately at home in his new environment, was soon learning from Uncle Gikita or Kimo or Dabu how to whittle fish spears. And almost immediately he began to follow his relatives into the forest to learn the exciting secrets of blowgunning. From his hammock he would watch Kimo make the poison from the bark of the *oonda* vine for darts to be used in hunting. On his return from trips downriver or into the forest, he would join the others who were hungrily dipping into the family meal of fish or monkey spread invitingly on banana leaves on the ground.

Akawo was proud of her grandson. She cooked special pieces of fish or meat for him, roasted his bananas, and made his yuca drink. She wanted him to be a good Auca, so she made him a *komi* from jungle cotton and wound the thin cord around his hips, as she had done for each of her own children. Akawo announced that soon it would be time to start making holes in his earlobes for the big balsa plugs.

In addition to hunting and fishing, Sammy had a very special job. He played the Auca phonograph records, which had arrived in time to be taken to the Tiwaeno with the returning party. To the amazement of the Aucas, Dayuma's son could wind the "foreigners' thing," place a disc on it, and make it talk in their language!

The first time the group heard the box speaking about God, they were stunned into complete silence. Rachel had learned long before from Dayuma that Aucas said the least about the things that impressed them most. Dyuwi and Oba followed every word. Kimo stopped making poison darts and came closer to see the records turning. He folded his muscular arms, leaned against a post, and riveted his eyes on the talking box. Akawo forgot her work, squatted down on the ground beside the phonograph, and listened closely. The four records were played over and over again.

"Now listen, all of you come. Come and sit down and listen," was the message from the box. "Listen, and then believing, live. Long, long ago God created. The sun, stars, and moon He created... then the wild hogs and the jaguars....

" 'Now what shall I create? I will create a man. I will take dry earth and breathe into it and create a man who will live....'

"After the temptation in the garden of Eden and the entrance of sin into the world, God said, 'Now what will I do that they may live well? Now in exchange, I will send My Son. Yes, He will become like a child and be born.' Then He died high on a tree; His very good blood dripped.

"This is the way God speaks. Our ancestors just said, 'God created'—then they didn't remember any more....' "

Uncle Gikita paid little attention to the foreigners' thing with its new message. "When I die, I will just become worms," he said. His interest lay in "stuffing himself on wild hog" rather than hearing God's carving. But Akawo listened as long as anyone would wind the box.

Sammy taught Dyuwi how to operate the machine. Then when no one else was around, Dyuwi would often listen raptly. One day he heard the record say, "If we don't believe in Jesus, our hearts are black like the blackest night. If we believe in Jesus, our hearts become like light. Do you understand?"

"I understand!" Dyuwi answered vigorously.

Gimari liked to listen, and she, too, learned to operate the foreigners' thing. Clumsily at first, she changed the needles and beamed with great satisfaction when she could make the box talk. She always brought baby Bai to hear. As he squatted on the ground, his eyes would brighten each time he recognized the name of Jesus spoken on the records.

In the evening when the men came home from hunting, they would gather around to hear the records over and over again. They seemed never to tire of the repetition of the messages.

The story of the Gadarene commanded great attention. Dayuma's version of the miracle held her people spellbound, just as Rachel's account had moved Dayuma when she first heard it.

"The devils are afraid of Jesus," the machine said. The listeners hardly moved a muscle.

The owner of the pigs that were drowned by the devils was very angry. He said to Jesus, "Jesus, why did You come here? You said to all of my pigs, 'Die!'—and they *died!*"

The Aucas always broke into a hearty laugh when they heard how the pigs ran down into the water and were drowned. But the lesson of the power of Jesus over the devils often provoked serious discussion around the fires afterward.

A summary of the Ten Commandments covered one side of a record, and gave them something new to think about.

"God says that you should not spear people," was the solemn message. "Even if you don't spear them yourself, but tell others to spear, that is sin."

Kimo and Sammy became close companions, especially as the Quichua-speaking boy quickly began to speak the language of his forest family. Sammy was able to tell his relatives much about the outside world. As the time drew near for Rachel to go to Limoncocha, he told Kimo of the foreigners there. Kimo and Dawa had wanted to go to the base ever since Mintaka and Maengamo returned with a favorable report.

It had been almost two years since Kimo had attempted a glimpse of the world beyond the forest. At that time, the guns of the Quichuas had frightened him back when he reached the Oglán. Dawa had actually gone out with Mintaka and Maengamo for a few brief hours, but ran back into the forest to join her husband.

Even when Dayuma went to the Tiwaeno the first time alone with Mintaka and Maengamo, before the foreign women had ventured in, apprehension still filled the forest. Kimo and Minkayi had been wary of the contact made with the outside world. However, after hearing from Dayuma about the outside as well as about God's carving, Kimo had resolved to receive the foreigners peaceably and to build a shelter for them. He had believed Dayuma's words that the white women would bring good and not evil to the Auca forest. However, others had warned him of bad days ahead.

"The hut you build will become your grave," they had predicted morosely. But Kimo was not to be dissuaded. He had promised Dayuma that he would build a hut for the newcomers, and he did.

When Rachel and Dayuma and Sammy began to make definite plans for Limoncocha, Kimo and Dawa decided to accept Dayuma's invitation to accompany them. She had been encouraging them to see for themselves how the good foreigners lived. Aucas would be welcome, she said.

In September when the party started for Limoncocha, Betty Elliot and her daughter, Valerie, left for a visit to her parents' home in the United States.

Rachel and the Aucas flew from Arajuno to Limoncocha in the JAARS plane. Kimo and Dawa were glad to be back on the ground. Kimo admitted that his first ride was a frightening experience. He flew very high, and the jungle trees below seemed far, far down. He saw the long, winding Napo River with clusters of huts or Quichua Indians along its banks.

At Limoncocha, Kimo saw many amazing foreigners' things, including a tractor and a motor scooter. His first view of the tractor at work was an awesome sight. He heard the roar of the "wood-bee on the ground," and ran out to see what was happening. He kept a safe distance under big trees at the edge of a clearing as he watched the mechanical monster pushing huge tree stumps and logs before it, and even knocking down small trees. The strength of the tractor driven by the foreman of the base impressed Kimo.

In a few minutes the tractor had accomplished more than a complete day's work for an Auca. He said with a hearty laugh, "I wish that the man pushing that wood-bee would beat me. Then I could work like that on the Tiwaeno!" He was remembering when Grandfather Karae often came back from a full day of chopping trees or clearing weeds and, following an Auca custom, would pick up the leather thong and beat the bare backs and arms of the youths. In this way they, too, would grow up to be good workers.

But Kimo's chief delight was to watch the JAARS pilots and mechanics in the hangar, working on the "skeleton and skins" of the wood-bees. He marveled at the ability of the men to "create" the bees that flew so high.

"Kimo went to the base with certain misgivings," Rachel recalls. "For the first three weeks he would not walk alone the short distance from our house to the hangar, though he very much wanted to see the airplane 'created.' There were too many Quichua Indians around. Although they had no firearms, he was afraid. But before the month was up, Kimo would stay at the hangar alone with our pilots and mechanics and even carried on quite a monologue in Auca."

Dayuma proudly escorted Kimo and Dawa around the base, where they shared the happy life of the foreigners living there. They went canoeing and fishing on the lake and ate contentedly around their ground fire outside Rachel's thatched hut. They even learned to play the hilarious game of volleyball, which the foreigners enjoyed each day at sunset. Awkward at first, Kimo quickly learned to coordinate his strong muscles to the unfamiliar sport and send the ball over the net.

But the high point for the group was the teaching from God's carving, held each evening under the thatched roof. Dayuma and Rachel would lead in Auca, or Catherine Peeke in Quichua. Catherine, who had enjoyed working with Rachel at Hacienda Ila, was now visiting her and the Aucas at Limoncocha. When she taught Dayuma and Sammy in Quichua, Dayuma would interpret the message into Auca for Kimo and Dawa.

For the first time in their lives, Kimo and Dawa observed the habits of foreign men who loved God. They heard them pray. They watched them gathering also to hear God's carving in their language.

After a moon at Limoncocha, the day came for the Auca group to return to the Tiwaeno. An hour before takeoff time, Kimo and his friend Sammy were at the hangar, standing by the Helioplane, laden with their blowguns, dart holders, and small bundles of foreigners' things acquired at the base. Kimo wore a broad, happy smile as he said good-bye to the foreign friends who surrounded the plane as the party left.

From Arajuno the party again took to the now-familiar forest trail. When they arrived on the Tiwaeno a few days later, all fifty-six of the Auca family group were on hand to hear Kimo's report. Many things had impressed him, but one observation especially gripped Kimo: the difference between "foreigners who loved God" and those who did not. When traders from the Napo River or Quichuas from surrounding villages had come to the base for medical treatment or on business, Kimo had asked curiously, "Do they love

God?"Very often the answer had been negative. He had watched the handful of Christian Quichuas who worked at the base, as well as other outsiders.

"Those who believed in God were happy—you could tell by their faces," was Kimo's conclusion. "Those who did not believe in God had sad faces. They live black."

"They looked like bats!" Dawa added.

"The Quichuas who live on the Napo River heard God's carving a long time ago," Kimo told his people. "But they have not all believed. We have just heard God's carving. If we had heard long ago, fast we would have believed."

Kimo had made another observation as he flew over the vast jungle. "We cannot hide from the wood-bees that fly over us," he told his people. "From the sky the smoke from the fires is clearly seen."

Kimo had noticed at the base that on Sunday the Quichua Indians first went to hear God's carving, and then hunted for food in the forest. Back on the Tiwaeno, he followed the same practice and encouraged others to do likewise. One Sunday, Dabu was more eager to hunt than to listen to the early-morning lesson. Kimo said he would listen to God, then go hunting. He asked God to help him find meat quickly. After the gathering, he took his blowgun and went into the forest. Early in the afternoon he came home with a happy smile and a collection of toucans, wild cranes, and gate monkeys. Dabu returned later with nothing. Kimo had a simple explanation for his success:

God said to the toucan, "You go sit on the tree by the trail and wait for Kimo"—and the bird did. The animals were just waiting to be carried home by Kimo for hungry mouths in the clearing.

Happy-go-lucky Minkayi listened with interest to Kimo's view of God's carving. Even Nimonga was saying that he would "plant lots of yuca and live for a long time on the Tiwaeno." But although he was friendly enough to live together with them, he had little interest in the new way of life that Kimo and others wanted to follow.

As Rachel listened to the Aucas around the fires at night or in the hammocks during the day, the typical pattern of conversation was being varied by talk about God's carving. References to attacks from the downriver people bore a new emphasis.

"If they spear us," Rachel heard Dawa tell Dayuma one day, "we will just die and go to be with Jesus."

Dayuma often agreed with the gloomy predictions concerning the fate of the Tiwaeno group. In fact, she told Rachel that when she was speared, she wanted Rachel to take Sammy as her own son. One day, Rachel felt impelled to channel Dayuma's thoughts in another direction.

"Dayuma," she said, "why do you always talk about being killed by the downriver people? Why don't we ask God to keep us from being speared until we finish God's carving for your people?"

Dubious at first, Dayuma began to include this request in her prayers. God *could* protect them. In fact, He could make a way for His carving to reach the impossible downriver people who were still angrily throwing spears at wood-bees that chanced to fly overhead.

"If God says 'no,' they won't be able to touch us," Dawa chimed in one day.

Foreigners—good and bad—were always a topic of conversation. Once when Rachel joined Dawa and Dayuma, she realized they had been talking about the foreigners killed on the Curaray. At the Tiwaeno, Rachel had heard that Dawa and Mintaka and Akawo were with the five Auca men who killed the foreigners, but she had never interrogated the eyewitnesses. Now Dawa was recalling impressions.

"After the first one was speared, the other foreigners shot their 'things' into the air," she said, "but they did not shoot our men. When all their shots were gone, our men just speared the rest of them."

Now Rachel knew how the bullet hole was made in Nate's plane.

Dawa's recounting later encouraged Rachel to ask Akawo about the death of her brother Nate.

"Mother Akawo, you saw my little brother killed. Would you tell me about it?"

With tears and many gestures, the woman began to describe the agony of her son Nampa, who was crushed by a powerful boa and later died.

"Crying with great pain, 'your little brother' Nampa died," she sobbed in conclusion.

It was then that Rachel realized Akawo was speaking to her as Dayuma's big sister. "Your little brother" meant acceptance into Akawo's family. She inquired no further concerning her own brother's death.

As part of the family circle, Rachel learned more about Auca beliefs and legends. She filled in many details of stories Dayuma had told her through the years. One day she asked Dayuma for further information about the Auca creation and flood story. "Ask Uncle Gikita," she replied. "He knows the stories better than anyone else."

Indeed, Uncle Gikita proved to be an excellent storyteller. He seemed glad to repeat the story for Rachel, who handed him the microphone. Uncle Gikita seemed amused as he examined it and wondered if the midget machine could really "hear" him. He was elated when he heard his own voice coming back from the box.

"The big rain came and covered the land," he began. "Then the Aucas heard the floodwaters coming. 'Watch out!' they called. If they had not lived well, the water fast took them, then they didn't live.

" 'We have lived well,' some cried, and the big water flowed around them on one side and the other. There they just stood on a little piece of land.

"A man and his wife said, 'We will cut off a rotted log,' and they hollowed it out. Then they took beeswax and put it on the ends, patting and patting it on. They put in all their food, yuca stalks, banana cuttings, sweet potatoes, corn, peanuts. Then they took their fire stick and crawled in. They closed the hole with beeswax. The waters carried them far, far downriver. Swirling with the current, they floated to where 'downriver' ends. Then the log got caught in the underbrush, and they could no longer hear the bumping against it. 'Let's make just a tiny hole. If the waters come in and drown us, we will die.' They made just a small hole. There was no water! The sun was shining. They opened their log, and took out their food. They began to clear weeds to plant their fields.

"Then two others said to them, 'Who are you?'

" 'We are Aucas,' they replied. 'We were about to be drowned upriver, then we came here.' "

At this point, old Uncle Gikita stopped to laugh heartily.

"Then two red-headed woodpeckers came," he resumed. "Flying right straight through the big tree trunks, they left holes in them. 'What do they do? They are strong,' the Aucas said. In the morning, waking up, they saw the two red-headed woodpeckers swooping down and pulling up the earth with their beaks.

" 'The big woodpecker is creating the mountains and the hills,' they said. That's what our ancestors said, Nimu. They were talking wild," chuckled old Gikita.

"Talking wild? What do you mean, Uncle Gikita?" asked Rachel.

"Now we know better," he laughed. "Dayuma has come and told us that God created *everything*! Now we know the straight story."

# Epilogue

## Tiwaeno—Without Spears

Tiwaeno, lying at the bend of Chonta Palm River for which it was named, was the first settled Waorani community in Ecuador. Located upriver at the headwaters of Amazon tributaries not far from the foot of the Andes, Tiwaeno was now clearly visible from the air. The Waorani people here made no attempt to hide from foreigners who flew over in planes.

Against a backdrop of lush, matted jungle lay a grassy airstrip the size of a football field. The airstrip formed the center of the progressive Indian settlement. Large thatched houses stood clumped together at one end of the elliptical bald spot on the jungle floor. The airstrip, adequate only for skilled jungle pilots, had opened an aerial gateway to the foreigners' world for the first time.

Air service spelled progress for the work on several fronts. In May 1961, Kimo and Minkayi and their wives flew with Rachel and Dayuma to Wycliffe's jungle center at Limoncocha on the Napo River for a linguistic workshop under the direction of Dr. Kenneth Pike. A milestone was reached when the Waorani alphabet was officially approved, and Rachel was encouraged by Pike to undertake the translation of the Gospel of Mark.

In August 1962, the airstrip served a special purpose. Now Dayuma was to become the bride of Komi, son of Gikita. Excitement was in the air when the plane, piloted by Wycliffe's Don Smith, landed in the village. Soon Don was informed that he would participate in the wedding.

"But what shall I do?" he asked Rachel, realizing that he lacked the practice necessary for such an occasion.

"Just do whatever the men do and follow their lead," she told him.

Don galloped around the airstrip with the Waorani men in a traditional wedding dance that ended under a thatched-hut roof, where Dayuma sat beaming in a hammock. The willing groom was plunked down beside her. The men chanted the wedding song, Don squatting beside Uncle Gikita. "Now you are married!" they sang. When the song was ended, Dyuwi and Don asked the Lord to bless the marriage.

The following year the airstrip served a more somber purpose when the small plane became an ambulance for Dayuma. The birth of baby Nancy "Hummingbird," begun in Auca fashion in a hammock, became complicated. The birth was completed at Shell Mera at HCJB's hospital. Nancy became the first Waorani birth to be officially registered in Ecuador.

Early in 1965, the Gospel of Mark was finally published. Catherine Peeke, who had joined Rachel in the task, wrote of the difficulties in translating abstract concepts. "There are deficiencies in vocabulary because the Waorani have lived without any cognizance of the civilized world around them. In this category lie the concepts of buying and selling, or even of trading; any form of specialized labor, as a carpenter, fisherman, teacher, sower; any religious or governmental organization; any concept of village or city; any idea of law, trial, or authority. Coins are 'metal fish scales.' The fact that Dayuma has had experience in the outside world alleviates the situation quite drastically."

Great excitement filled the village when the JAARS plane with its precious cargo of God's carving landed on the tiny airstrip. Special guests were SIL's Ecuador director Don Johnson and his wife, Helen, and Steve and Phil Saint, sons of Nate Saint who had visited their aunt in Tiwaeno on several occasions.

Following the dedication of the Gospel of Mark, plans were made for Steve to spend part of the summer in Tiwaeno. Steve's sister, Kathy, now almost sixteen, wrote Rachel of her desire to be baptized by Waorani believers. Steve also expressed his desire to be baptized. When his mother learned of the plans, she suggested that the entire Saint family visit Palm Beach.

## Baptism on Palm Beach

Marj and Kathy arrived from Quito, and the trip through the jungle to the Curaray River was planned.

Kimo and Dyuwi led the way through a tangled forest festooned with flowering vines and gigantic, feathery ferns. The Saint children bounded ahead with the Indians, laughing and shouting Waorani phrases. Dayuma, who had learned some Spanish, chatted with Marj Saint. Rachel was delighted to be once again with Nate's family.

At the Curaray, the group boarded canoes for Palm Beach. They poled downstream until mid-afternoon, when a downpour drove them to shelter at a spot on the river where Gikita had previously built fishing shacks. There they found dry wood for a fire and made coffee. When the rain ended, they continued toward Palm Beach.

Late in the afternoon, the group rounded a normal-looking bend in the river to behold what Kimo solemnly pointed out to be Palm Beach.

Dawa had witnessed the massacre in 1956. She had watched Dayuma's mother, Akawo, distract the foreigners as Gikita and the younger killers prepared to attack. One by one the foreigners had fallen. Although they fired shots into the air, warning the Indians that they had means of defense, they chose to be killed by spears.

Deep remorse had followed when through Dayuma her people learned that the foreigners had come in peace, desiring to bring them God's carving. Meditating sadly on the death of the men, Dawa had suddenly brightened. "Dying, we will see them again, and seeing them, we will be happy."

Now nine years later, Dawa and her husband were at Palm Beach again, together with Nate's widow, Marj, and her three children. Kimo's concern for their comfort was a touching indication of transformation. He and Dyuwi made palm-leaf shelters for the night, and spread large leaves on the jungle floor for beds. Through the night the men watched the rain-swollen river rise to a dangerous height, and alerted the group to move to higher ground.

At dawn the next morning, the group gathered by the river as Kimo explained to Steve and Kathy and two Waorani teenage candidates for baptism the need to leave sin and live truly for God.

They sang an appropriate hymn in their Waorani language, and Dayuma read the verses concerning baptism from the first chapter of Mark.

Closing the ceremony, Kimo prayed, "Lord, long ago, not knowing You, we sinned *right here*. Now, believing in You, we are going to meet You in the air!"

Kimo and Dyuwi then led the group from the beach down a short jungle trail to the site of the five graves.

Rachel, Marj, and the other four widows had circled over the scene of death in a U.S. Army plane in 1956. Now two of the Palm Beach killers stood with Marj and Rachel by the graves. Canopied by a luxurious leafy ceiling, the group sang in the silent forest the hymn the five men and their families had sung just before the men left for Palm Beach the last time:

> We rest on Thee, our Shield and Defender,
> Thine is the battle, Thine shall be the praise;
> When passing through the gates of pearly splendor,
> Victors, we rest with Thee in endless days.

"Tears held back for years flowed freely, at least for the Saint family," Rachel wrote later. "As I looked up, I saw above the graves five red jungle flowers, standing straight and tall, with the sun filtering through that gorgeous forest."

## Polio!

As the message of God's carving gradually changed the lives of the Tiwaeno dwellers, the welfare of their downriver relatives became their chief concern. Downriver, they were still spearing each other, as well as outsiders. In answer to prayer for a peaceful contact, a young downriver relative, Oncaye, fled to the outside for refuge, much as Dayuma had years before. Eventually, she found her way to Tiwaeno. With Oncaye's help, downriver settlements were located from the air.

In partnership with the Tiwaeno believers, Pilot Don Smith made contact using microphones hidden in native baskets and dropped on downriver clearings. Elusive and apprehensive, the downriver people were slow to respond, fearing a foreigners' trap. By patient contacts, two groups from downriver had come to Tiwaeno by 1968—12 in one group, and 92 in the next. The original settlement had grown from 56 in 1958 at the time of contact, to 104. With the influx of 104 from downriver, the village had now doubled again.

Catherine Peeke, who had completed her Ph.D. in linguistics at Indiana University, returned to Tiwaeno to help Rachel cope with the newcomers. Further contacts were made with Waoranis on "the ridge," another unreached group of relatives.

In August 1969, news reached Tiwaeno that Waoranis living on the Curaray were falling ill, with severe flu symptoms. Dawa, skilled in administering medications, left Tiwaeno, taking her supplies with her. She reported by radio that a young man had died, drooling at the mouth and with partial paralysis. His mother came to Tiwaeno, and within a short time she, too, had died.

Rachel conferred with Lois Pederson, the Wycliffe nurse at Limoncocha. Upon hearing the symptoms, Lois suggested the possibility of polio. On September 24, she and Dr. Wallace Swanson of the HCJB Shell Mera Hospital were flown to Tiwaeno and confirmed the diagnosis. Two patients were taken to the hospital, where they died. Fourteen more patients died in Tiwaeno within two weeks, and many others were ill.

Friends in the United States and Ecuador joined in helping the stricken community, providing vaccine and equipment, including crutches and wheelchairs. Nurses came from the United States to help. Rosi Jung, a German Wycliffe member and a graduate midwife, assisted in the polio ward at Shell Mera. Eventually, she joined Rachel and Catherine as a permanent translation team member.

Finally, in November 1969, flights that had been suspended because of the polio epidemic were resumed. At that time Toña, a gifted Waorani teacher, began calling from the plane to relatives below. After receiving assurance from his relatives on the ground, he made a risky jump from a helicopter to a group of ridge relatives. Equipped with a two-way radio, he called each day to report progress: "Today I told them of the Creator God…. Today I told them that God had an only Son…." His last call came one day in June 1970. He was never heard from again.

Eventually, Dayuma and her family moved from Tiwaeno to Toñampade—"Toña's Place"—named for the first Waorani martyr. It was located on the Curaray near Palm Beach. Catherine and Rosi continued to live in Tiwaeno as they pressed ahead on the translation of the New Testament.

Toñampade, connected to the outside world by air, became a thriving school center as more Waoranis joined the group there and the number of children increased. The Ecuadorian government, encouraged by the dramatic change in the Waoranis, cooperated in the training of bilingual schoolteachers and the building of schools. To augment the Wycliffe team, a talented literacy teacher, Pat Kelly, joined in the education effort. Air transportation facilitated the supervision of reading programs in Tiwaeno, Toñampade, and other new settlements.

## "God's Carving" Completed

June 7, 1992, marked a day of great rejoicing as a small plane bearing precious cargo landed at Tiwaeno. "God's Carving," the New Testament in the Waorani language, was being delivered to Dayuma's people.

Mary Sargent, one of the original team, prayerfully recalled events leading to this day of triumph:

"I think of all the struggles the years have meant, Father, of all the prayers You have answered; of all the lives around the world You have touched through one event, of the way You prepared 'the seed of the martyrs' to be fruitful.

"I remember the night I knew that Dayuma believed in You. I think she was believing bit by bit, but that night Rachel had told her the story of Lazarus, and Dayuma was telling it back. I was watching, and I saw You in Dayuma's eyes; I knew she believed."

Mary recalls the Scripture dedication program:

"It began with the school kids lining up by rows for the raising of the flag and the singing of the national anthem. In a culture where to sing is to chant, there was an inimitable sound of small voices juggling tones just outside the realm of chant and barely within the confines of melody. We followed the children inside the schoolhouse where the program continued. We were moved as we listened to Tanye read from the Waorani New Testament. Dayuma led in the prayer of dedication. The final hymn was listed as 'Hymn of Hope,' which we who were visitors tried to chant along with the Waorani."

A second dedication held in Shell Mera was attended by many foreigners. Rachel's joy was made complete by a strong representation of the Saint family: Kathy Saint Drown and her son Daron; Stephen Saint, his wife, Ginny, sons Shaun, James, and Jesse, and daughter Stephenie; Phil Saint, his wife, Karla, and sons Karl and Daniel; and Sam Saint's granddaughter, Debbie Klang.

Following the ceremony, the whole Saint clan flew to Rachel's home in Toñampade. For Nate's grandchildren, it was a time of discovery; for his children, a time of remembrance. As the Waoranis led the whole family to nearby Palm Beach, a sense of closure comforted Rachel, through tears of joy.

## Rachel's Graduation

Rachel's life reached a turning point in 1993. Cancer had been diagnosed, and her strength was failing. She continued to work in Toñampade, eager to complete the illustrated Bible story book in the Waorani language. Her eyesight had diminished, although cataract surgery had restored some sight.

On a trip to the United States in the summer of 1994, she conferred with her physician in Florida. The physician confirmed the spread of the malignancy. Having expressed a strong desire to die in Ecuador, she was given permission to return. By November her strength had failed rapidly, and friends in Quito volunteered to care for her. Jim Smith, pastor of the English-speaking evangelical church in Quito, and his wife, Sharon, were often by Rachel's side in her final days. With waning strength, sensing that her departure was near, Rachel turned to Jim and Sharon. "Well," she said, "I guess I'd better go to heaven so you can get back to work." She then began to pray almost continuously, in Waorani and Spanish, as Sharon held her hand. On November 11, 1994, she gave Sharon's hand a final squeeze.

Steve Saint flew to Ecuador to arrange for his aunt's burial in Toñampade. He described his arrival in the village: "The Waorani gathered closely around the plane and peered in all the windows to be sure that we had in fact brought 'Nimu' back to them. There was a great deal of crying. Dayuma and Dawa sobbed brokenheartedly. They wanted to see Aunt Rachel one last time, so they took her body to Dayuma's house, where the women gave her a last-minute 'fixing up.' Her body had been lovingly dressed and prepared by a national couple in her Quito church. When we had rested her head on a pillow, and had tied just the right scarf around her face, the women allowed the men to move Aunt Rachel's body to the church."

Dyuwi, Minkayi, and Kimo, three of the Palm Beach killers, were at the funeral service. Komi, Dayuma's husband, summarized what Nimu had taught him. Minkayi said, "She called us her brothers. She told us how to believe. Now she is in heaven. Happy and laughing, she is in heaven. Only those who believe go to heaven." Kimo said, "God is building a house for all of us, and that's where we'll see Nimu again."

Dawa reminded the group that when Nimu's brother came and was killed by them, they didn't believe anything: "Only when Nimu came did we begin to believe."

Jim Smith concluded the service with a short message taken from the Gospel of John. Then the Waorani family carried Nimu in her coffin to the hole they had dug beside the church in front of the memorial plaque commemorating the death of Pete, Roger, Ed, Jim, and Nate. After a song was sung, Dyuwi prayed, and then the grave was filled.

## Steve Saint Returns

In January 1995, Steve was back in the Ecuadorian jungle, in response to an invitation the Waoranis extended at the time of Rachel's burial. The Indians led him on a trail from Toñampade to Nimompade, a new location, which was a tortuous eight and a half hours of constant climbing and descending.

The distant jungle location of Nimompade was to be the center of a new venture. Steve reviewed the decision that led him, his wife, Ginny, and their four children to pioneer in a remote spot in the Ecuadorian jungle:

"I visited Ecuador four times last year. Each time I went, the Waorani asked me if I would go to live with them when Aunt

Rachel died. These were the people I had known and loved since I was a little boy, hunting and fishing with them while I lived with Aunt Rachel. These were the people that Dad had died for, and that Aunt Rachel had lived for. They were people whose faith had strengthened my own. Whose lives of simple obedience had been an example to me. Two of the men had baptized Kathy and me."

Steve believed that lasting help for the Waorani would come through someone who knew their culture and language. He had a working knowledge of both. He also believed that the person needed to be an Ecuadorian. Steve had just received the renewal of his Ecuadorian citizenship for life, and the Ecuadorian government had passed a new law recognizing the legal status of dual citizens. As God's leading became clearer to him, he helped Ginny overcome her anxiety. All four of their kids were immediately enthusiastic about the possibility of going.

After the decision to move to Ecuador was made, plans for building an airstrip at the new site soon got under way. A team of helpers volunteered to build a jungle home and a clinic. Supplies were then flown in as the family took up residence. Steve wrote:

"For Ginny, I think the biggest adjustment is the lack of privacy. Our house, though quite nice by jungle standards, is very open to outside inspection. The outside walls are more window than wall. The floor and inside walls were built with boards that had been part of a growing tree as recently as two or three hours before taking their place in our construction. As they are drying we are left with fairly substantial 'inspection cracks' between the boards so that the entire community can monitor our activities."

Medical help in the new location represented a new effort to improve the lives of the Waorani. The clinic was always busy, as Waorani health promoters were trained. Steve now flew patients in his plane to the Nimompade clinic, instead of to the distant Shell Mera hospital.

At the end of the summer the two oldest boys, James and Shaun, left to attend college in Florida. Jesse and Stephenie, high schoolers, continued their classes by homeschooling in the jungle.

Old Uncle Gikita came to see the new center. Steve described his reaction:

"He held my shoulders and pulled my head right up to his and said, 'I've heard what you are doing here in Nimompade. You take care of sick people, and that is good. But you must show my grandchildren how to live God's way so that living happily we can all be together someday in heaven. Write it down now so they won't forget. I'm an old man now and I want to die, but I want my grandchildren and their children to come to heaven."

# Glossary
### (1960 Edition)

(S., Spanish; Q., Quichua; A., Auca)

ACHIOTE (S., ah-chee-*oh*-teh) This decorative shrub, the urucu or bixa (*Bixa orellana*), has a pink blossom and a fragrance akin to that of the apple blossom. The Aucas paint their faces with the soft red pulp which coats the spicy seeds.

AMUNGA (A., ah-*moon*-gah) The musmuki (*Aotus infulatus*), a nocturnal monkey. A foot in length, it has a very long tail, and eyes encircled in black. The Aucas hunt the amunga in hollow logs, where it sleeps by day.

AUCA (Q., *ah*-oo-cah) The name "Auca" is used interchangeably in Ecuador with the term "Aushiri," also of Indian origin (possibly Cofan or Záparo). It is a term used by the Quichua Indians to designate savage, pagan, or barbarian groups of Indians. In Spanish and English the term has been narrowed to indicate the one savage tribe or group of tribes which controls the southeastern jungle of Ecuador, the area between the Napo and the Curaray Rivers.

AWAEMAE (A., ah-*wam*-a) The walis (Q.) fruit, similar to the wild cherry.

BALSA (S., *bal*-sah) The balsa or corkwood tree (*Ochroma piscatoria*. etc.), whose light-weight wood is used by the Aucas to make earplugs and other objects, especially the balsa raft for river transportation.

BARBASCO (S., bar-*bas*-coh) Barbasco (*Lonchocarpus nicou*). A shrub whose roots are pounded and cast into a dammed-up stream to drug the fish, so that they are easily caught by hand or with spears.

BOA (*bo*-ah) The boa constrictor, an anaconda which is said to attain to the length of 39 feet in Auca territory. Connected with witchcraft in Auca beliefs; antidote after killing a boa is to drink an infusion of hot pepper. The water boa is more feared by the Aucas than the land boa because of its greater size, and they rarely attempt to kill it because of the disadvantage of its being in the water.

BOGI (A., *bo*-gee) The machín (S.) monkey. The Aucas referred to white foreigners as "like *bogi* monkeys" whose palms are white.

BUYUGA (A. boo-*voo*-gah) A rodent, the *chambu* (Q.), smallest variety of agouti (*Dasyprocta*). Has the appearance of a tail-less squirrel and lives in the ground.

CHAMBIRA (Q., cham-*bee*-rah) The tucuma (*Astrocaryum tucumá*) fiber, taken from terminal tender leaf shoots of this palm.

CHONTA (Q., *chon*-tah) The chonta or pejibaye palm (*Guilielma gasipaes* or *G. speciosa*). This palm is planted for its prolific (though seasonal) vegetable-like fruit, called *chontaruro* (Q.). The especially hard cortex of the chonta palm trunk is considered the best material for Auca spears; was formerly the material used for making heavy, tooth-studded clubs, and for creating a substitute *machete* (S.) or long bush-knife. The latter was given a sharp edge by cutting and filing with a stone. Of all the palmhearts available, only the heart of the chonta palm is appreciated by the Aucas.

COCUYO (Q., coh-*coo*-yoh) A light-bearing snap beetle. One inch or longer, bearing light cells on abdomen which emit a large red light when the beetle is in flight, and small light organs on either side of the thorax which may produce green lights when the insect is crawling among the bushes. Both lights shine constantly rather than intermittently, and both seem to vary in intensity or become extinguished at the will of the creature.

CUSHMA (S., *coosh*-mah) A loose-fitting, full-length robe worn by the men of several Amazonian tribes; made simply of one or two lengths of cloth joined at sides and shoulder, with a slit for the head.

GAGAI (A., gah-*gah*-ee) The evening star.

GAMUNGA (A., gah-*moon*-gah) The kinkajou or honey-bear (*Cercoleptes caudivolvus*). A carnivorous nocturnal mammal with pre-hensile tail.

GATA (A., *gah*-tah) The woolly monkey, a favorite for pets.

GIKARI (A., gee-*car*-ee) The Veracruz ivory-billed woodpecker, scarlet crested.

GIMlNIWAE (A., ghee-mee-*nee*-wa) The *uchu putu* (Q.) or "pepper kapok" tree, which bears a dark-colored, worthless kapok. The giant tree is anchored by great buttressed roots which fan out to form natural booths. Orioles customarily hang their long nests from the high arched branches of this tree.

GYAEGYAE (A., *gyag*-ya) The *challulla* (Q.) river fish of Ecuador and Peru.

HUITO (Q., *wee*-toh) The edible fruit of the genipa (*Genipa americana*) tree yields a clear juice which is colorless on application to the skin, but soon turns black. Used for decorative body painting.

ILA (Q., *ee*-lah) The *ojé* (S.), a giant among jungle trees (*Ficus anthelminthicas*). Hacienda Ila takes its name from a small stream which runs through the property; the stream presumably bears the name of the formerly abundant ila tree.

IMIÑI (A., ee-*meen*-yee) A scorpion, whose curved abdomen is terminated in a poisonous sting.

IWA (A., *ee*-wah ) The howler monkey (*Mycetes*).

IYATAI (A., ee-yah-*tah*-ee) A slender, red-gold ant of about three-fourths of an inch in length. A member of the household of the leaf-cutting Atta ants.

JAGUAR (S., *jag*-war) A carnivorous, spotted "Great Cat," one of several large varieties known in Spanish as *tigre*.

KAPOK (*kay*-pahk) A tropical tree of the Bombacaceae family (*Bombax ceiba*), source of the cottonlike kapok fiber. The tall tree grows along the rivers, bears its seed in a dark pod surrounded by the kapok fiber. Since the tree is thorny, trees are often cut for harvesting the fiber, but some trees are scaled by the Aucas.

KOMI (A., *coh*-mee) A "belt" of loosely twisted cotton strings worn around the hips by the Aucas—men, women, and children.

LEAF-CUTTING ANT The "sauba" or parasol ant (*Atta cephalotes*). This refers to the worker caste, whose business it is to cut and carry large leaf fragments to act as fertilizer in their underground fungus gardens.

MACAW (mah-*caw*) Refers to one of the large blue-backed *guacamayos* (S.) of the parrot family, especially the scarlet macaw and the golden macaw.

MAÑI (A., *mahn*-yee) The *Dinoponera gigantea*. one of the world's largest ants, about an inch and one quarter in length. The sting of this giant mañi ant causes severe discomfort for several hours, comparable to that produced by the sting of some scorpions.

MIIMO (A., me-*ee*-moh) The *chichico* (Q.), tiniest of the monkeys found in this jungle. Body not over eight inches.

MU (A., moo) The *macana panga* (Q.), a low-growing leaf which the Aucas use to intersperse rows of a larger palm leaf in thatching. It is also used to spread on the dirt floor of the Auca huts to serve as tablecloth, serving dish, and plate.

NIMU (A., *nee*-moo) The Auca word for "star."

OCELOT (ah-*se*-laht) A carnivorous "small cat," which is here used to refer to any of the number of varieties known in Spanish as *tigrillo*.

OMUYAEMAE (A., oh-moo-*yam*-ma) A jungle fruit similar to the peach. The Aucas call this fruit the *moipa omuyaemae*, referring to the time when Moipa and Gikita found a tree of the ripe omuyaemae fruit, ate several, and Moipa suddenly got a seed stuck in his throat.

OONDA (A., oh-*ohn*-dah) The curare poison, made from *pala wasca* (Q.) or "flat vine," the *Strychnos toxifera*. The tips of blowgun darts are coated with curare for killing small animals.

ORIENTE (S., oh-ree-*en*-tay) The popular name for the eastern jungles of Ecuador.

PAENAE (A., *pan*-na) The agouti (*Dasyproctus aguti*). Edible rodent which attains to almost two feet in length. Accused of being a great manioc thief.

PATRÓN (S., pah-*tron*) Landlord or employer of Indians. They work for, owe their allegiance to, and claim protection from this landowner.

PIRO (S., *pee*-roh) A member tribe of the Arawak language family. The main concentration is located along the Urubamba River in Peru, and there are other widely scattered villages of Piros in other sections of southeast Peru and possibly in Bolivia and Brazil.

PITOWAE (A., pee-*toh*-wa) The *Euterpe edulis* palm, whose giant pinnate leaves are used by the Aucas as thatching; this was the common roofing material used on the large Auca huts when the tribe was more numerous. This leaf is used in conjunction with another, the *mu* (A.), which is doubled over the pitowae to make an especially tight roof. The oily fruit has the appearance of a ripe olive, but a milder flavor and less flesh. Used by the Aucas for food and for hair oil.

PLÁTANO ( S., *plah*-tah-noh ) General term embracing the banana (*Muse paradisiaca sapientum*), or the plantain (*Muse paradisiaca normalis*), one of the real staples of the Aucas, which is cooked as a vegetable, whether green or ripe; the ripe fruit is also the basis of an unfermented drink.

POGANTA (S., poh-*gahn*-tah) A simple headband, formed of one strip of the cream-colored fresh leaf-shoot of the *ramos* (Q.) palm. The headband is often decorated with spots of red *achiote* (S.) paint.

QUICHUA (*kee*-choo-ah) The most numerous Indian group in western South America; the dominant Indian language, handed down from the Inca conquerors. Dialects of Quichua are spoken in jungle as well as highland areas.

SHAPRA (*shah*-prah) A member tribe of the Candoshi or Murato group of head-shrinking jungle Indians; north Peru, in the region of Lake Rimachi.

SHIGRA (Q., *shee*-grah) The carrying net, made in varying sizes, is woven by jungle Indians from tucuma palm fiber. It is interlaced in one piece with an elongated strap of closer weave, to serve as a tumpline.

SPIDER MONKEY According to the *Encyclopedia Britannica*, "a group of tropical American monkeys known to zoologists as *Ateles*. They take their English name from the slimness of the body, the elongated limbs, and the long tail, the under surface of the prehensile extremity of which is naked. The thumb is rudimentary or wanting. Their long coarse hair and the broader partition between the nostrils distinguishes them from the woolly spider monkeys (*Brachyteles*). The species are arboreal."

TAPIR (*tay*-per) A hoofed, herb-eating mammal (*genus Tapirus*), called "jungle cow" by the Quichuas, for it attains to the proportions of a small cow.

TARIRI (tah-*ree*-ree) A contemporary Shapra Indian chief, region of Lake Rimachi, northern Peru.

TIPA (A., *tee*-pah) The *tarapoto* (Q.) palm (*Ireartea ventricosa*). The fruit borne is a tiny coconut, not eaten by human beings, but is one of the chief foods of the jungle deer. The broad pinnate leaf is used for temporary shelters. The trunk is commonly used for uprights in Auca huts; it is also flattened by splitting, utilized as wide springy boards for flooring.

TOUCAN (too-*cahn*) Tropical perching birds (*Rhamphastidae*). The species to which most common reference is made here, boasts of a large curved beak almost as long as its body, black with light blue pattern.

UVILLA ( S., oo-*veel*-yah ) The uvilla ( Spanish for "little grape") fruit has a single stone, but is much like the grape in flavor, consistency, and skin. It is borne in great clusters on the crown of branches spreading high on the slender trunk of the uvilla tree.

WANIMU (A., wah-*nee*-moo) The morning star.

WIIWA (A., we-*ee*-wah) The *pingullu* (Q.) or "slender bamboo" bird. A tiny brown-black bird, its whistle is like that of a melodious flute.

WILD PIG The peccary (*Tayassuidae*) of tropical America. Two varieties are recognized here: the collared peccary and the white-lipped peccary. The latter is the larger variety, and customarily runs in bands.

WIÑATARA (A., ween-yah-*tah*-rah) The name given by the Aucas to another Auca group who speak a slightly different dialect.

WIPITA (A., wee-*pee*-tah) The *mintal* (Q.) tree, whose red wood is grated and boiled in water to form a brilliant red lacquer-like liquid. This is used to paint areas of the foot affected by a fungus which resembles interdigital ringworm. The red paint is also used to dye tucuma fiber cords in preparation for weaving hammocks.

YARINA (S., yah-*ree*-nah) Edible, refreshing fruit is borne at eye level, enclosed in a mass of hard, bristly shells. Its rather fine pinnate leaf is woven for a durable thatch by the Aucas. Unsuitable for a quickly-constructed, temporary shelter.

YUCA (S., *yoo*-cah) The manioc or cassava (*Manihot palmata, utilíssima, esculenta,* etc.). The several varieties cultivated by the Aucas are all edible upon being cooked. After boiling, a staple is made by pounding and masticating the root to form a mass which is mixed with water as desired, and drunk unfermented by the Aucas. It is wrapped in leaves and carried on trips.

ZÁPARO (Q., *sah*-pah-roh) A near-extinct language family of jungle Indians, scattered along rivers in northern Peru and southern Ecuador. Known by various family names, river names, and dialect names. The Quichua name "Záparo" designates a certain type of covered basket, woven by the Záparo Indians.

# Pronunciation of Names

Adyibae (ah-*dyee*-ba)
Aentyaeri (an-*tyar*-ree)
Aepi (*ap*-pee)
Aka (*ah*-cah)
Akawo (ah-*cah*-woh)
Ana (*ah*-nah)
Awaenga (ah-*wan*-gah)
Awaengai (ah-wan-*gah*-ee)
Awañita (ah-wahn-*yee*-tah)
Bai (*bah*-ee)
Biba (*bee*-bah)
Bibanga (bee-*bahn*-gah)
Boika (*bwee*-cah)
Dabu (*dah*-boo)
Dawa (*dah*-wah)
Dayo (*dah*-yoh)
Dayuma (dah-*yoo*-mah)
Dika (*dee*-cah)
Dyiko (*dyee*-coh)
Dyiwanga (dyee-*wahn*-gah)
Dyuwi (*dyoo*-wee)
Gaba (*gah*-bah)
Gakamo (gah-*cah*-moh)
Gami (*gah*-mee)
Gikita (ghee-*kee*-tah)
Gimari (ghee-*mah*-ree)
Gingata (gheeng-*ah*-tah)
Gomoki (goh-*moh*-kee)
Ima (*ee*-mah)
Ipa (*ee*-pah)
Ipanai (ee-pah-*nah*-ee)
Itaeka (*ee*-tac-ca)
Jacinta (ha-*seen*-tah)
Karae (*cah*-ra)
Kimo (*kee*-moh)

Kinta (*keen*-tah)
Kipa (*kee*-pah)
Kiwa (*kee*-wah)
Komi (*coh*-mee)
Kominkagi (coh-meen-*cah*-gee)
Koni (*coh*-nee)
Maengamo (man-*gah*-moh)
Maruja (mah-*roo*-ha)
Miguel (mee-*gel*)
Miipu (me-*ee*-poo)
Mima (*mee*-mah)
Mingi (*meen*-gee)
Miñi (meen-*yee*)
Miñimo (meen-*yee*-moh)
Minkayi (meen-*cah*-yee)
Mintaka (*meen*-tah-cah)
Moipa (*mwee*-pah)
Monga (*mohn*-gah)
Naenkiwi (nan-*kee*-wee)
Ñaeno (*nyan*-no)
Nambai (nahm-*bah*-ee)
Ñamae (*nyah*-ma)
Nampa (*nahm*-pah)
Natani (nah-*tah*-nee)
Nimonga (nee-*mohn*-gah)
Nimu (*nee*-moo)
Nombo (*nohm*-boh)
Oba (*oh*-bah)
Obi (*oh*-bee)
Olimpia (oh-*leem*-pee-ah)
Omaena (oh-*man*-nah)
Omaenkiri (oh-man-*kee*-ree)
Omaenga (oh-*mahn*-gah)
Omiñia (oh-meen-*yee*-ah)
Ompora (ohm-*poh*-rah)

Onae (*oh*-na)
Onaenga (*oh*-nan-gah)
Pa (pah)
Tamaenta (tah-*man*-ta)
Tamaya (tah-*mah*-yah)
Tañi (*tahn*-yee)
Tipayae (tee-*pah*-ya)
Toña (*tohn*-yah)
Tuwa (*too*-wah)
Tyaemae (*tya*-ma)
Tyaento (*tyan*-toh)
Tyaenyae (*tyan*-ya)
Umi (*oo*-mee)

Wagingamo (wah-geen-*gah*-moh)
Wamoñi (wah-*mohn*-yee)
Wani (*wah*-nee)
Warikamo (wah-ree-*cah*-moh)
Wato (*wah*-toh)
Wawae (*wah*-wa)
Wiba (*wee*-bah)
Wiika (*wee*-cah)
Wiña (*ween*-ya)
Wiñaemi (ween-*ya*-mee)
Wiwa (*we*-wah)
Yaeti (*ya*-tee)

The stripped and deserted plane of the five missionaries who were murdered by Waorani Indians

Marj and Rachel Saint on the trail to the beach for the baptism of Nate and Marj's children

Gikita putting barbs on his spear, the type of Spear used to kill the missionaries

Rachel helping Dayuma read a portion of the Waorani Bible to
Kimo (l) and Duywi (r), two of the men who killed the missionaries

Jesse Saint and Mincaye, one
of those who killed
Jesse's grandfather

Elisabeth Elliot and Rachel Saint
in Ecuador

Dayuma

Waorani man with a New
Testament in his own language

The Saint family: James, Steve, Ginny, Jesse, Stephenie and Shaun. Steve
and Ginny currently work among the Waorani tribe with their two
youngest children who are continuing their education by homeschooling.